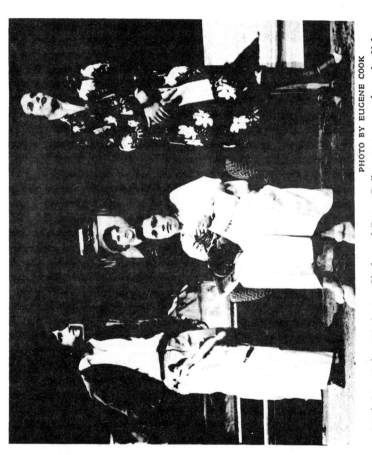

Mark Linn-Baker, Katherine Clarke and Darcy Pulliam in a scene from the Yale Repertory Theatre production of "Dentity Crisis."

THE NATURE AND PURPOSE OF THE UNIVERSE

DEATH COMES TO US ALL, MARY AGNES

'DENTITY CRISIS

THREE SHORT PLAYS BY CHRISTOPHER DURANG

★

★

DRAMATISTS
PLAY SERVICE
INC.

CONTENTS

THE NATURE
AND PURPOSE
OF THE UNIVERSE

THE NATURE AND PURPOSE OF THE UNIVERSE was presented by the Direct Theatre at the Wonder Horse Theatre in New York on February 21, 1979. The production was directed by Allen R. Belknap, setting by Jonathan Arkin, lighting by Richard Winkler, costumes by Giva Taylor. The cast was as follows:

RONALD, an agent of God .... Jeff Brooks
ELAINE MAY ALCOTT, an agent of God .... Caroline Kava
STEVE MANN .... Tom Bade
ELEANOR MANN .... Ellen Greene
DONALD MANN .... Ethan Phillips
ANDY MANN .... Eric Weitz
GARY MANN .... Chris Ceraso
COACH GRIFFIN .... Robert Blumenfeld
RALPH .... T. A. Taylor
FR. HEMMER .... T. A. Taylor
THE POPE .... Robert Blumenfeld

(The roles of Ralph and Fr. Hemmer, and of Coach Griffin and the Pope, may be doubled.)

A "radio play" version of the play was presented by the Direct Theatre in September, 1975, directed by Allen R. Belknap and Yannis Simonides. Due to the "radio" concept, there was more doubling among the men's roles. (Further information on the radio version may be found at the end of the script.) The cast of this version was as follows:

RONALD, an agent of God .... Justin Rashid
ELAINE, an agent of God .... Lynnie Godfrey
STEVE MANN .... James Nisbet Clark
ELEANOR MANN .... Anne De Salvo
ANDY, COACH, FR. HEMMER .... David Wilborn
DONALD, RALPH .... Nick Mariano
GARY, THE POPE .... Lars Kampmann

(The non-radio version requires 2 women, 7 men. The radio version requires 2 women, 5 men.)

SETTING

There are two ways to set this play.

The first is to set it recognizably in the messy middle class home of Eleanor and Steven Mann. Kitchen area, kitchen table and chairs Stage Right; living area with TV and small sofa Center Stage; desk and chair of living area Stage Left. (This presumes a fairly wide stage. With a narrower stage, the TV Center area and desk Left area can be merged into one area; the sofa can become a chair.)

This home is not presented too realistically. For instance, though Eleanor should have a frying pan, she should have no stove; it's better that she mime using one. And in the scenes set outside the home, there should be no attempt to actually change the set. For instance, the school scene of Miss Mansfield's office should be placed at the desk in the house (with Center Stage and Stage Right blacked out). The nightclub in Iceland can be the kitchen table with a cloth thrown over it (or even no cloth); if snow should fall, it falls in the kitchen.

Because Ronald sets the scene in his narration, the audience is fairly willing to accept the change of scenes without actual set alteration; and thematically there is something appropriate in all of the scenes taking place in the home.

The other alternative is to split the stage ⅔, ⅓. The Right ⅔ is the Mann home; you need the kitchen, living area—the kitchen table and chairs, a TV, an arm chair or sofa. The Stage Left ⅓ would be "Ronald and Elaine's area," an all-purpose area outside the home where Ronald and Elaine go about their "agent of God" business. The area would need a sturdy table and two chairs. The table, with prop additions at the designer's discretion, would be made to represent Sister Annie's office; the office of Miss Mansfield; the table in the nightclub in Iceland; and the sacrificial table at the end of the play. The Pope's speaking in Hoboken would also be set there. Throughout the play, whichever set you use, there should be a chair Stage Left for Ronald to sit in and watch the action whenever he is not in a scene or is not addressing the audience.

> SCENE: *A kitchen-living room setting, not too elaborate and flexible enough to accommodate easy changes. A few chairs, a kitchen table set for breakfast. Cereal boxes and the like.*
>
> *Enter Ronald, an agent of God. He is dressed neatly in*

7

a suit and tie, or perhaps in a tuxedo. On his arm is Elaine, another agent of God; she is dressed in an attractive red or black evening gown. They walk toward the audience, smiling, as if inviting them to an especially elegant social event.

RONALD. The Nature and Purpose of the Universe. Chapter One. It was an ordinary Tuesday morning, much like any other Tuesday morning. (*Elaine now exits, having completed her greeting function.*) The frost was on the pumpkin and a nip was in the air. It was an ordinary Tuesday morning, much like any other Tuesday morning. Steve and Eleanor Mann were just getting up. Eleanor was still crying softly into her bathrobe because her oldest son was a dope pusher, and her middle son was a homosexual and wore purple scarves, and her youngest son had recently lost his penis in a strange McReilly's reaper accident. (*Ronald goes and sits in his chair L.; out of the action. He watches. Enter Eleanor and Steve Mann. Eleanor looks bedraggled, and carries a frying pan and spatula; she stands by the kitchen table and scrambles eggs; she cries softly into a dish towel. Stove, eggs not necessary. Steve, in a suit, sits at the table, reading a newspaper and drinking coffee. For a while there's just the scrambling, the reading, the quiet crying.*)

STEVE. Eleanor! Why are you crying? You just got up.

ELEANOR. Oh, Steve. I don't understand it. Not any of it. Our house is worth forty-five thousand dollars. Where did it all start to go wrong? (*Enter Donald, about 25, seedy and vicious.*)

DONALD. Hey, Mom, where's my spare hypodermic?

ELEANOR. Oh, Steven. Speak to your son.

STEVE. I saw it in the hall closet.

DONALD. God damn it. (*He exits. Enter Andy, about fourteen, wearing short pants with a large white bandage covering the crotch of the pants.*)

ANDY. Good morning, Mom. Good morning, Dad. (*Eleanor looks at him and, overcome with grief, cries into a dish towel.*)

STEVE. Good morning, son. How's the boy?

ANDY. Okay. (*Enter Donald.*)

DONALD. God damn it! The needle's not there! Now where is it? One of you must have taken it. Who was it?

ELEANOR. (*Sobbing.*) Oh, Donald, why must we live like this?

DONALD. (*Hurls her to the ground.*) Shut up, you stupid

drudge! Did you throw my hypodermic out? Did you, you slut? Slattern! Trollop! Tramp!

ELEANOR. Steven! Don't let him treat me this way!

STEVE. Donald, have a little patience with your mother please.

DONALD. You threw the needle out, didn't you, bitch? (*He kicks her.*)

ELEANOR. (*Screams.*) You shouldn't take drugs! You shouldn't sell drugs! We'll all be arrested!

ANDY. We need more sugar, Mom, for the cereal.

DONALD. What do you know? You're going to pay me for that needle and I'm going to kill you if you take any of my things ever again! (*He kicks her. She screams.*)

ELEANOR. Steven!

STEVE. Don't despair, Ellie. Have faith. God provides.

ELEANOR. I know, but look what He's provided!

STEVE. (*Furious.*) Don't you dare to talk against God, you whore of Babylon. (*He kicks her.*) Do you want the children not to believe in God?

ELEANOR. Oh, Steve, please! Let me finish making the eggs.

STEVE. What sort of example is that?

ANDY. We don't believe in God, Dad. Ever since that earthquake in Peru.

STEVE. You see what you've done, Pig?

ELEANOR. I didn't cause the earthquake! Oh, Steve. Let me finish the eggs.

DONALD. Hurry up, I'm hungry. (*The sons and father go calmly back to eating, Eleanor gets up from the floor, cries into the dish towel, and starts scrambling the eggs again. There is silence except for the eggs and her whimpering.*)

STEVE. (*After awhile.*) Eleanor, don't snivel. It's depressing.

ELEANOR. I'm sorry, Steven. (*Enter Gary, the middle son, dressed entirely in purple.*)

GARY. Good morning, Dad. Good morning, Donald. Good morning, Andy. (*He kisses his father and brothers on the cheek.*)

ELEANOR. Don't you say hello to your mother?

GARY. (*Chilly, doesn't like her.*) How are you, Eleanor?

ELEANOR. Oh, Gary. Gary, Gary. (*Gary starts to nuzzle Andy's shoulder, and then kiss behind his ears. Eleanor, after a bit.*) Gary, Stop it! Your brother has no genitals! Leave him alone. (*Donald kicks over the table.*)

DONALD. Can we have no peace in the morning? Is there no civilization left anywhere in this stupid house? What kind of town is this? What kind of people are these? (*He hurls his mother to the ground.*)

ELEANOR. Steven, help me! Help! (*Enter Ronald. Action freezes. Then actors exit, except for Ronald.*)

RONALD. The Nature and Purpose of the Universe. Chapter 2. It was an ordinary Tuesday morning, just like any other Tuesday morning. There was much for Eleanor to do. There was the cleaning to do, and the beds to be made, and the meals to be prepared so that she could keep home nice for her men. Andy went off to school, Gary off for a short cruise in the park, Steve went off to his job, and Donald went off to scrape and save, pimp and push. God assigns my friend Elaine to impersonate a next-door neighbor who upsets Eleanor. (*Ronald sits in his chair. Enter Eleanor with a vacuum cleaner. Eleanor tries to turn the vacuum on, but it won't work. She starts to cry.*)

ELEANOR. (*On her knees.*) Oh, please, God, please let my vacuum cleaner work. Please. And I promise I won't complain about my sons. Just please let my household appliances work. I don't care about the electric toothbrush, but I need the vacuum cleaner and the washing machine and the (*She sobs.*) refrigerator. Oh, please God! Please! Let my car start again and I promise I'll pick up hitchhikers even if they beat me with chains because I know that some of them are your angels sent in disguise to test me, I know this, my husband Steve tells me it's so, and he's much more religious than I am. I'm just an unworthy woman. Oh, God, help me. (*Enter Elaine May Alcott, dressed as a housewife. She drags a little girl behind her. The little girl is apparently entirely unconscious. The little girl is best played by a doll.*)

ELAINE. (*Furious.*) Don't you ever answer your door bell, Mrs. Mann? Do you always ignore your neighbors?

ELEANOR. Oh, Mrs. Ackerman, I'm sorry. I didn't hear the bell. Can I get you coffee or . . . What's the matter with your daughter?

ELAINE. Well might you ask, Mrs. Mann. I found her in the bathroom this morning, passed out next to the john, and I found this hypodermic stuck in her little arm. (*She whips hypodermic out of her purse.*) See this, Mrs. Mann?

ELEANOR. Oh, Mrs. Ackerman, how horrible!

ELAINE. Horrible, she says. You hear that, God? The dope

10

pusher's mother is horrified. (*Elaine jabs Eleanor's arm with the hypodermic.*)

ELEANOR. (*Screams.*) Oh, my God, you've punctured me.

ELAINE. (*Mimicking.*) Oh, my God, you've punctured me. Damn right I've punctured you. What about my daughter? Do you know how much weekly allowance we have to give Caroline to feed her habit? Fifty dollars a week. You hear that, Mrs. Mann? We have to pay my hop head daughter fifty dollars a week, all of which goes to your hateful, sick son.

ELEANOR. Oh, Mrs. Ackerman.

ELAINE. Your family is the bane of Maplewood, Mrs. Mann. My husband has been attacked in the garage by your pansy son twice now, and just last week we found your little son's penis in our driveway. My little Bobby was going to use it for fish bait until I took it away from him. Do you think I like to live in this atmosphere of sickness, Mrs. Mann? Do you think I want to live near your horrible family?

ELEANOR. Oh, Mrs. Ackerman, I know how you must feel. But do you think we might possibly have my son's penis back?

ELAINE. Certainly not! I put it right down the garbage disposal. I don't want your family's private parts hanging around my kitchen. (*Elaine jabs Eleanor with the hypodermic again.*)

ELEANOR. Mrs. Ackerman, please. I'm bleeding.

ELAINE. Bleeding, she says. You hear that, God? My little daughter Caroline is o.d.ing and Mrs. Mann is complaining about a few punctures. (*Screaming.*) What about my daughter? I want some reparation. Reparation, Mrs. Mann!

ELEANOR. Oh, Mrs. Ackerman, what can I say?

ELAINE. Give me your color TV! I want your color television.

ELEANOR. Oh no, please. Donald would beat me. He watches TV all the time.

ELAINE. I don't care what he does. I just know that I'm taking your television set or I'm calling the police.

ELEANOR. Please, please, Mrs. Ackerman. (*Elaine picks up the television set.*)

ELAINE. (*Shouting.*) KEEP YOUR HORRIBLE FAMILY AWAY FROM ME, DO YOU HEAR? Do you hear? (*She exits with television, leaving little Caroline behind.*)

ELEANOR. There, there, Caroline, it's all right. (*Enter Ronald. Action freezes, then actors exit.*)

RONALD. The Nature and Purpose of the Universe. Chapter 3.

It was an ordinary Tuesday morning, but oh God, thought Eleanor, what has happened over the years? All my hopes dashed, she thought, all my illusions crushed. I remember how happy I was in high school, playing the lead in a Chekhov play. What one was it, I wonder? And while Eleanor thought these despairing thoughts, she did the wash and baked a cake. And while Eleanor prayed to God, God was busy communicating a message to Steven about the New Pope. God's instrument on earth is again my friend Elaine May Alcott, whom God this time assigns to masquerade as Sister Annie De Maupassant, the radical nun of Bernardsville. *(Ronald sits. Enter Elaine dressed as a nun. Since Elaine has little time to change costumes, her costumes should be minimal. In this case, a nun's veil. Elaine sits at a desk, blesses a cigarette, then smokes it. Enter Steve.)*

ELAINE. How do you do, Mr. Mann. I am Sister Annie De Maupassant, the radical nun of Bernardsville.

STEVE. I have heard much of your reputation, Sister.

ELAINE. And I of yours, Mr. Mann. I am told that you are one of the most thoughtful and brilliant of Catholic laymen within a radius of five dioceses. The Jesuits speak well of you.

STEVE. I am humbled by your thinking well of me.

ELAINE. But enough of this small talk. We are here on more important matters. Something is awry in Rome. The Pope is not the proper Pope. He is a fraud. He is not the Deity's choice.

STEVE. Sister Annie De Maupassant, what can this mean? You mean Pope Paul is not a proper Pope?

ELAINE. Pope Paul is a false Pope. He speaks with the Papal wee wee.

STEVE. As bad as that?

ELAINE. I fear so.

STEVE. What must be done?

ELAINE. In a few weeks Pope Paul is coming to New Jersey to bless the air in Weehawken. God has communicated to me that we must spirit him away, reveal him as a fraud, and instate the true Pope in his proper place. Only then will the Church be able to gain its rightful and dominant place in the world.

STEVE. Sister Annie De Maupassant, you may certainly depend on me.

ELAINE. God bless the laity! Thank you, Mr. Mann, I knew I could. My agents will get in touch with you soon. Simply continue

12

your life as you normally would, stay close to the sacraments, and make ready for the Holy Spirit.

STEVE. Sister Annie De Maupassant, I have one question. Has God perhaps revealed to you who the true Pope is?

ELAINE. Yes, Mr. Mann, He has.

STEVE. Who is it to be? (*Elaine stands on her desk.*)

ELAINE. Mr. Mann, it is I, Sister Annie De Maupassant, who is the true and only Pope. (*She throws a handful of glitter into the air and stamps her foot in triumph. Then she opens her mouth and lets out a high, continuous shrieking sound, while her tongue flies in and out of her mouth. She places her hand on her throat, in surprise, as if she has no control over the noises she is making. The noises stop, and she speaks.*) Bon jour, Jean. Comment ca va? Auf wiedersehn. Oh my God, I'm speaking in tongues. (*She shrieks again, her tongue going in and out, it's a gibberish sound, half sung, half screamed. Then she speaks again.*) Moo goo gai pan. (*Swedish.*) Yo. Inga Swenson gunnar cheese. (*Shrieks again. Has Steve help her exit. Then while she is exiting:*) Flores, flores para los muertos. (*She and Steve exit. Ronald addresses the audi- again.*)

RONALD. The Nature and Purpose of the Universe. Chapter 4. The sun hit its zenith shortly after noon that day, just as Gary and his new friend scuttled behind a bush in the park. It was a Tuesday like any other Tuesday, except that Eleanor got a call from Andy's junior high school principal. It seems that Andy had upset his athletic teacher. God assigns Elaine to play the role of the principal's secretary, and the athletic coach plays himself. (*Ronald retires to his seat. Enter Elaine, Coach Griffin, and Andy. Elaine sits at a desk, ripping up papers and/or shooting rubber bands into the air. Andy's shirt is off, and Coach Griffin is whipping him on the floor. Enter Eleanor, carrying a full laundry basket.*)

ELEANOR. Oh, dear, oh, dear. What is the matter?

ELAINE. I'm sorry to interrupt your busy day, Mrs. Mann, but we have a little problem here. (*Offers her hand, gracious.*) I'm Miss Mansfield, Mr. Watson's secretary. Mr. Watson is on sabbatical this semester, and in his absence I have complete power. (*Looking around room, cheerfully awed.*) I don't know what to do with it all, really.

ANDY. (*Being whipped.*) Mommy!

ELAINE. (*Charming.*) Oh, I'm sorry. Coach Griffin, please don't inflict any more corporal punishment on Master Mann right now. (*To Eleanor.*) Discipline is a delicate thing. Mrs. Mann, I'm going to be frank. We've all been worried about Andrew in school lately.

COACH. I won't have no boy without a male organ in my gym class.

ELEANOR. That seems to me prejudiced.

COACH. If he doesn't have an organ, he should be on the girls' side. I'm not having no girl in my gym class.

ELAINE. (*Smiles.*) You see our problem.

ELEANOR. Well, I guess there's nothing I can say. Can Andrew be exempted from gym?

COACH. Certainly not.

ELAINE. We have our rules.

ELEANOR. Well I guess he'll have to have gym with the girls then.

COACH. Damn right.

ELAINE. (*Pleased.*) I'm glad that's settled.

COACH. And he can't wear an athletic supporter either.

ELEANOR. I'm sure he wouldn't want to, Coach Griffin. Mr. Griffin, I only hope that someday you are mangled by a McReilly's reaper, and then I hope you shall have more sympathy for people without organs.

ELAINE. Please, let us remain ladies and gentlemen.

ELEANOR. Might I go now?

ELAINE. I'm afraid we have another complaint to deal with, from the Mother's Cake Committee of the PTA. I have here a letter from Mrs. Samuel Fredericks which I must read to you. (*Reciting.*) Dear Miss Mansfield, I am shaken . . .

ELEANOR. Where is the letter?

ELAINE. (*Smiles.*) I've committed it to memory. Dear Miss Mansfield, I am shaken and upset. At our otherwise successful Mother's Cake Sale at the children's playground the other day, our festivities were disturbed by the actions of a certain young man who my daughter says was Andrew Mann. This young boy had the temerity to approach our Mother's Cake Counter where he proceeded to undo his pants and to expose himself to the baking mothers present. We were all appalled. There was nothing there. New paragraph. Now, Miss Mansfield, I am as much in favor of charity and kindness as the next mother, but enough is enough! I have been sick to my stomach all day, and expect to be so 'for much of tomorrow. Surely there must be a fit punishment for this crime, Miss Mansfield, for as our prisons attest, crime is encouraged by leniency. I leave this matter in your capable hands. Sincerely, Mrs. Samuel Fredericks, 31 Club Drive, Maplewood. (*Pause.*) Have you anything to say, Andrew?

ANDY. (*Softly.*) I hate school.

ELAINE. All children think they hate school. No, my task is to do the right thing, to perpetrate the correct punishment. So I've decided that to symbolize the ungentlemanly nature of Andrew's behavior he will be required to wear girls' clothing for one month, at which time I will reconsider his case.

ELEANOR. (*Concerned.*) Do you think that that will help him realize the wrongness of his action?

ELAINE. I don't know. But if he doesn't expose himself again, I shall feel we have succeeded. (*Lowering her voice.*) Exhibitionism of a sexual nature must be checked early, Mrs. Mann. Repression is a gift from God, and we must honor it as such.

ELEANOR. I worry that such punishment might be harmful.

ELAINE. Well, time will tell. Oh, and, by the way, Mrs. Mann, I'm afraid that Mrs. Fredericks requested that you return your PTA membership card and that your car be denied use of the school parking lot. Since parents are frequently partly to blame for the failings of their children, I think that this is only just. Thank you for coming, Mrs. Mann. I've enjoyed meeting you.

ELEANOR. Miss Mansfield, I can only apologize from the depth of my heart to you, and to you, Coach Griffin, for the pain and anguish my son Andrew has given you. And I only hope that never again will I be made to feel as embarassed and humiliated by a member of my family, and I beg you all to forgive me. (*She exits with her wash.*)

ANDY. Mommy! (*Coach whips him again, Elaine rips papers, perhaps all in rhythm. Enter Ronald. Action freezes, actors exit.*)

RONALD. The Nature and Purpose of the Universe. Chapter 5. It was an ordinary Tuesday afternoon, just like any other Tuesday afternoon, and Donald was doing so well that he had no more rooms to send his girls to, so he brought Crystal home. God assigns my friend Elaine to play Crystal. (*Exits. Enter Eleanor, still with the wash. Enter Donald and Elaine, who is dressed as a prostitute.*)

DONALD. Now look, Mom, there's no more room in the city so

Crystal's gonna meet her trick here, and she's gonna use your room.

ELEANOR. Oh, Donald, please.

DONALD. Look, can it, bitch. (*He pushes her slightly.*) I'm going to watch some . . . WHERE'S THE TV?

ELEANOR. Oh Donald!

ELAINE. Jesus.

DONALD. Where is the friggin' television?

ELEANOR. Donald, your language. (*He pushes her to the ground.*)

DONALD. (*Hissing.*) Where is it?

ELEANOR. Mrs. Ackerman took it in reparation.

DONALD. Who is Mrs. Ackerman?

ELEANOR. She lives down the street. You sell her little daughter drugs.

DONALD. Your story better be true. I'll be back. (*Exits.*)

ELAINE. (*Cheap dame voice.*) Your son's very violent.

ELEANOR. It was that year we lived in Union that did it. Donald used to be such a quiet boy, but the other children were so rough in Union. He had to learn how to defend himself. They used to fight with Coke bottles and power saws.

ELAINE. (*Getting on the ground next to her.*) You know, if you didn't have such dish pan features, you could almost be attractive, honey.

ELEANOR. Oh, dear God. (*Elaine inches closer.*)

ELAINE. Have you ever made it with another woman?

ELEANOR. Life Magazine was right! You are all lesbians!

ELAINE. Hey, come on, relax.

ELEANOR. Get away from me! Steve! Donald! Where are you? (*Elaine tackles Eleanor. Eleanor screams. Enter Coach Griffin. Elaine is on top of Eleanor.*)

COACH. Hey what's going on? Which one of you is Crystal?

ELAINE. (*Points to Eleanor.*) She is.

ELEANOR. No, I'm not.

ELAINE. See ya later, Crystal. (*Coach Griffin picks up Eleanor, carries her out as she screams. Enter Ronald.*)

RONALD. Hello, Elaine. How are you?

ELAINE. All right. Excuse me. I've got to go change. (*Exits.*)

RONALD. The Nature and Purpose of the Universe. Chapter 6. It no longer seemed an ordinary Tuesday to Eleanor. Coach Griffin's hot sweating body came down upon her with the force of

16

a thousand violins. The sun was like a hot pomegranate. Coach Griffin did degrading things to Eleanor, some of them very athletic. At the end of three hours, he kicked her very hard with his boot. (*Exits. Enter Eleanor, worn, and Coach Griffin.*)

COACH. That was lousy. That was among the worst I've ever had. Boy, you're lousy. You can tell Donald if he thinks I'm paying you for that, he's crazy. I should be paid for putting up with you, you aging slob. (*He spits on her, kicks her, exits.*)

ELEANOR. Oh, God, please let this day come to a close. Please! (*She sinks to the floor weeping. Enter Ronald. Ronald should be very sincere in the next scene.*)

RONALD. Excuse me. Your door was open. I'm the Fuller Brush Man.

ELEANOR. Please, please, leave me alone. I can't stand anymore.

RONALD. (*Takes her face in his hands.*) Eleanor, let me look at you.

ELEANOR. You know my name.

RONALD. Eleanor, I can see suffering in your eyes. Let me kiss them. (*He kisses her eyes lightly.*) You're a fine, noble woman Eleanor. God doesn't mean for you to suffer.

ELEANOR. He doesn't?

RONALD. No. He wants you to accept His will and be happy. (*His hand lightly caresses the top of her head.*)

ELEANOR. I do accept His will. (*Rather suddenly.*) Oh, please, please take me away from here. Far, far away.

RONALD. Yes, Eleanor. I will take you away. I will come for you next week.

ELEANOR. Oh, please. I must leave here.

RONALD. Eleanor, do not give up hope. I will take you away. Next week. (*He kisses her forehead, exits.*)

ELEANOR. Oh, thank you, God. Please let me be happy. I'll promise never to complain again. (*Enter Gary and a female impersonator.*)

GARY. Hello, Eleanor. I'm home.

ELEANOR. Oh, Gary. Gary. I'm so happy. You've brought home a young girl for me to meet. You don't know how happy this makes me. What's your name, dear?

FRIEND. Ralph.

ELEANOR. Oh, Gary. Gary, Gary.

GARY. Can it, Eleanor. Ralph and I are going to be up in your bedroom, so don't bother us.

ELEANOR. Please don't use my room. Gary, please!

GARY. Shut up!

RALPH. (*Politely.*) It was nice to meet you, Mrs. Mann. (*Exit Gary and Ralph. Enter Donald.*)

DONALD. There you are, you slut! I'll have you know Mrs. Ackerman's never heard of you or our television set, and I told her it figured cause you're a filthy liar anyway.

ELEANOR. Oh, Donald, please don't hit me. I'll ask your father to buy us all a new television.

DONALD. You'll pay for this, Mom. (*Kicks her a little.*) I'm kind of tired. Where's Crystal?

ELEANOR. I don't know. She must have left.

DONALD. Did she give you the money?

ELEANOR. No. There wasn't any money.

DONALD. What do you mean there wasn't any money? (*He hurls her to the ground.*)

ELEANOR. Don't hit me, Donald! That man thought I was Crystal and he raped me!

DONALD. Well, give me the money!

ELEANOR. He didn't give me any. He made me do awful things.

DONALD. PAY ME!

ELEANOR. Have mercy! Donald!

DONALD. Pay me, you slut! (*Enter Andy, dressed in a pink dress. He jumps rope.*)

ELEANOR. Donald, please! Andy, help me. Run for help! (*Andy keeps jumping rope.*)

DONALD. You pay me the money. Crystal gets thirty dollars, so cough up thirty.

ELEANOR. Donald, the bank is closed.

DONALD. I want it now. (*Donald is perched over his mother, more or less straddling her. He slaps her face lightly but continually.*)

ELEANOR. Stop! Help me! Help! Help!

DONALD. (*Slapping.*) You slut! Trollop! Tramp! (*Steve enters.*)

STEVE. I'm home, Eleanor. Is dinner ready? (*Slapping stops.*)

ELEANOR. (*Still under Donald.*) What, dear? I couldn't hear you.

STEVE. I said is dinner ready yet? Have you done your duty as a wife and cooked me and my sons dinner?

ELEANOR. Oh, Steve, I'm sorry. I haven't had time . . .

STEVE. What do you mean, you haven't had time? Great God

almighty! (*Steve pushes Donald away and gets on top of Eleanor, slapping her.*)

ELEANOR. But Steve I was raped!

STEVE. What kind of wife are you? You give my children a bad example, you don't make supper, you don't make beds, you're incompetent, you're a failure as a woman.

ELEANOR. Oh, God, help me. (*Enter Ronald—though "outside" of the set.*)

RONALD. Do not fear, Eleanor, I will save you in a week.

ELEANOR. Oh, God. (*A couple of lines before now, Elaine has entered, in her evening gown of the first scene, and she stands by Ronald's side. When Eleanor says "Oh God," Elaine picks up the phrase and sings it, thereby giving the entire company the starting note for the song they are about to sing.*)

ELAINE. (*Sings.*)

Oh God.

(*Ronald and Elaine now sing the hymn "O God, our Help in Ages Past"; the whole company joins in, not so much in response to Ronald and Elaine singing, but as if they were all overcome with an urge to sing a hymn at this time. Eleanor joins in the hymn also, on the last three lines, though still in much despair.*)

RONALD and ELAINE. (*And eventually everyone else.*) :
(*Sing.*)

O God, our help in ages past,
Our hope for years to come,
Our shelter from the stormy blast,
And our eternal home.

O God, our light against the dark,
We bow down to thy might,
Please help us understand thy bark,
Is far worse than thy bite.
(*An elaborate, pretty ending:*) Alleluia!

RONALD. The Nature and Purpose of the Universe. End of Part I. (*All exit except Ronald.*) The Nature and Purpose of the Universe. Chapter 7. It was Tuesday of the following week. It was an ordinary Tuesday, much like any other Tuesday. Truth was still beauty, and trudy booth . . . and yet still Eleanor woke with some hope; for today was the day that the Fuller Brush Man was supposed to save her. (*Enter actors: Steve, Andy, and Donald are eating breakfast. Andy has a bow in his hair. Enter Eleanor, followed by Gary and Ralph.)*

GARY. God damn it, Eleanor. Where is Ralph's bra?

ELEANOR. Gary, I said I just don't know.

DONALD. (*Throws a spoon.*) You're making too much noise.

GARY. Ralph says you've been trying on all his clothes.

ELEANOR. But, Gary, I have my own clothes.

RALPH. Oh. She doesn't like my clothes, she says.

GARY. Why do you insult my guests?

ELEANOR. I don't mean to, dear. Please believe me. I think Ralph's clothes are fine.

GARY. Well, where's his bra?

ELEANOR. I don't know, maybe Andy took it.

DONALD. Shut up!

GARY. (*To Andy.*) Did you take Ralph's bra? Did you?

ANDY. I put it back!

GARY. You little bastard!

RALPH. (*Grabbing the bow from Andy's hair.*) And that's my bow!

ANDY. It is not. Miss Mansfield gave it to me.

RALPH. He's taking my clothes!

GARY. (*To Andy.*) I'll kill you!

ELEANOR. (*Pulling Gary back.*) Don't hit him, he hasn't any genitals!

DONALD. SHUT UP! (*He kicks over the table.*) Why is there never any quiet in this house? Woman, it's your fault. You don't know how to run a house. Now pick up this table and clean up this mess. (*He stalks out. After a stunned silence, Andy starts to leave.*)

RALPH. (*To Gary.*) Let's get him! (*Andy screams, runs out.*)

ANDY. I don't have your stupid bra. (*Exits. Gary and Ralph run out after him.*)

ELEANOR. Gary! Wait! Don't touch his bandage!

STEVE. Eleanor, will you stay out of the boys' fights for God's sake? No wonder Andy's wearing dresses, you take on so. And pick up the table. Really, you are the worst wife and mother I've ever seen. You deserve an amateur hysterectomy.

ELEANOR. (*Truly horrified.*) Oh, Steven. Can't you please be nice to me?

STEVE. Don't snivel, Eleanor. (*Phone rings.*) Hello? Why, hello,

Sister Annie De Maupassant. I'm delighted to hear from you. Yes, I'm quite ready. Today's the day then. Alright. I'll be by for you shortly. Will we have any additional help? Oh, fine. I like a good Jesuit on a job. See you later, Sister Annie De Maupassant. Glory be to God. (*Hangs up.*)

ELEANOR. Is this some more Catholic Action work, Steve?

STEVE. Mind your business, woman. And clean this house. We're having ecclessiastic guests tonight, and I don't want them to know that I'm married to a pig.

ELEANOR. Oh, Steve, please be kind to me.

STEVE. Kneel down. (*She kneels.*) Leniency is not kindness, Eleanor. Overlooking faults is not a kindness. It is a sin. (*He kicks her, exits. Eleanor picks up the table, sets things straight. She brings the vacuum cleaner over toward table, tries to turn it on, it won't function. She starts to cry.*)

ELEANOR. Why doesn't the vacuum cleaner work? Oh, God. Oh, please God, let the fuller brush man come tonight. Please. I know You don't mean for me to be this unhappy. (*Phone rings.*) Hello? (*Ronald stands D., not holding a phone. Eleanor does not see him. The following scene is played mostly sincerely.*)

RONALD. (*Facing out.*) Hello, Eleanor. This is the Fuller Brush Man speaking.

ELEANOR. Oh, God, is it really you? Oh, help me. You will take me away tonight, won't you?

RONALD. Yes, Eleanor. I will. Are you sure you want to leave your family and home?

ELEANOR. Oh, please. I can't stand anymore. I'm bruised all over, but it is my heart that is truly wounded.

RONALD. Eleanor, Eleanor. I will come for you tonight at midnight. Have your bags packed.

ELEANOR. Oh I will! I will! But . . . please don't fail me. Hello? Hello? (*She hangs up. Eleanor exits.*)

RONALD. The Nature and Purpose of the Universe. Chapter 8. No one breathes much in Weehawken, New Jersey. The air drips with a veritable venereal disease of industrial waste. The atmosphere is slowly turning to sludge. It is very romantic. Pope Paul the Sixth was due to arrive in Weehawken that ordinary Tuesday morning, to bless the air. Meanwhile, Sister Annie De Maupassant and her Jesuit friend, Fr. Anthony Hemmer, meet with Steve to discuss their plans. God has assigned Elaine once more to the role of Sister Annie De Maupassant. Fr. Hemmer plays himself. (*Enter Elaine, dressed as a nun.*) Hello, Elaine. How are you finding the role of the radical nun of Bernardsville?

ELAINE. All right. I was surprised to see you getting in on things with that Fuller Brush Man routine.

RONALD. God works in strange and mysterious ways, Elaine. (*Ronald exits. Enter Steve and Fr. Anthony Hemmer.*)

ELAINE. Ah, there you are. Hurry. The pretender is about to enter. Fr. Anthony, I presume you've met Mr. Mann, the brilliant Catholic layman Fr. Obediah told you about.

FR. ANT. Yes I did. You certainly are a brilliant Catholic layman, sir.

STEVE. Why thank you, Father. I try.

ELAINE. Mr. Mann has some fascinating thoughts on the connection between the guitar folk Mass and the Albigensian heresy, but we have no time to discuss them now. I see the Papal Pretender fast approaching.

FR. ANT. We seem to be in luck. We seem to be the only ones here.

ELAINE. I'm not surprised. The Lord is thy shepherd. Ssssh. (*Enter Pope Paul, dressed in a gold outfit with gold slippers and a diamond tiara and droop earrings. He is accompanied by several monks [the other actors in monk robes, with cowls over their heads, covering their faces]; the monks enter in procession, singing in a Gregorian chant fashion:*)

MONKS. (*Singing.*)

Amo, amas, amat,

Amamus, amatis, amant.

(*Over and over as needed. The Pope follows behind them. When he nears* D., *he smiles graciously at the audience and then sings in a piercing, too high ecclesiastic voice, he has a small scrap of paper that he checks for the words.*)

POPE.

Agricula,

Agriculae,

Agriculae,

Agriculam,

Agricula, Ah-men.

Agriculae,

Agricularum,

22

Agriculis,
Agriculas,
Agriculis, Ah-men.

Sum es est,
Sumus, estis, sunt.

(*One of the monks leads the Pope away from the audience, and to the place where he is to speak.*) My brothers and sisters in Christ, we are gathered here in Weehawken in the face of this smog, which is a symbol of evil in the world, to stand up once again for all that is just and right and proper for salvation. God created man, and the word was made flesh, as it was in the beginning and in the middle and I feel faint. Help me. I feel faint. I am going to faint. Someone help me. I am faint. Where is the Curia? I shall faint. (*Two monks clutch the Pope on either side.*)

MONK. Take deep breaths, Your Holiness. (*The Pope breathes in deeply, giving out terrible gasps at the bad air. Elaine and Steve creep up behind the two monks and strangle them to death. The Pope is oblivious to this and shortly passes out due to all his deep breaths. Steve and Fr. Anthony pick the Pope up.*)

ELAINE. (*Crosses herself.*) All that I do I do for God! Forward march for the New Church! (*Enter Ronald. Action freezes, then actors exit.*)

RONALD. The Nature and Purpose of the Universe. Chapter 9. It was an ordinary day no longer. Eleanor looked at herself in the mirror and felt an inner joy. At least it was joy compared to what she usually felt. For tonight would be her redemption, her escape. For a few moments, she harbored the fear that something would go wrong, that the fuller brush man would not come, that her life would continue as a hell. Her packing is interrupted as God sends Elaine to impersonate the census lady. (*Enter Eleanor with a suitcase. Enter Elaine.*)

ELEANOR. Oh! You startled me.

ELAINE. CENSUS!

ELEANOR. What?

ELAINE. I am the census lady come to get you.

ELEANOR. What do you mean?

ELAINE. How many children do you have?

ELEANOR. Three.

ELAINE. Are you married?

ELEANOR. Yes.

ELAINE. Don't get uppity with me. This is a with-it world. You can never tell who's married nowadays. (*Shouts.*) WHAT DOES YOUR HUSBAND DO?

ELEANOR. Please don't shout.

ELAINE. I'm sorry. (*Shouts.*) WHAT DOES YOUR HUSBAND DO?

ELEANOR. He's a salesman.

ELAINE. I see. A salesman. Attention must be paid, my ass!

ELEANOR. What do you mean?

ELAINE. Does he have sex with you?

ELEANOR. Is this necessary for the census?

ELAINE. The census itself is not necessary, so your question is irrelevent. Do you have sex with your husband?

ELEANOR. I don't think that . . .

ELAINE. Answer the question.

ELEANOR. Yes, when he demands his rights by marriage.

ELAINE. What do you do?

ELEANOR. I don't see how this affects . . .

ELAINE. Do you have oral sex? Do you have anal sex? Do either of you use chains?

ELEANOR. I will not answer any of these . . .

ELAINE. Have you ever had nasal intercourse?

ELEANOR. I . . . don't think I know what it is.

ELAINE. Look at these. (*She takes some photos from her purse.*)

ELEANOR. (*Pushing photos away.*) I don't want to see any more.

ELAINE. Well, have you?

ELEANOR. Certainly not.

ELAINE. Does your husband do anything to your nose at all?

ELEANOR. No.

ELAINE. What do your sons do?

ELEANOR. My two oldest are presently unemployed, waiting to return to college, and my youngest is in the eighth grade.

ELAINE. Oh, is that so?

ELEANOR. Yes.

ELAINE. Really?

ELEANOR. Yes.

ELAINE. It is not!

ELEANOR. Yes, it is!

ELAINE. It is not. (*Shouting.*) You phony liar. Your oldest son pushes dope and is a pimp. I have here a signed affadavit from three hundred badly used women. (*She takes out the paper.*) And your second son is a homosexual. I have super 8 film of him. (*She takes out a roll of film.*) And your youngest son lost his penis in a reaping accident and I have here a signed statement attesting to that fact from the entire eighth grade girls' gym class. So don't try to fool me with your pathetic lies. Admit that you lead a lousy life. Do you know on a national scale of one to 800, you rank 92; and on a local scale you are 33, and on an international scale 106, and on an all-white scale 23, and on an all-black scale 640, and on a pink scale 16, and that your capability ranking places you in lowest percentile in the entire universe. It's a sad life I see before me, Mrs. Mann. You haven't any friends. None. Do you realize that you never call anybody up and that nobody ever calls you up? And that you're universally snubbed and pitied at PTA cocktail parties? And that your husband married you only because he had to, and your housekeeping is among the most slovenly on the eastern seaboard, and your physical appeal is in the lower quadrangle of the pentanglical scale—and that's not very high, Mrs. Mann—and that your children rank as among the foremost failed children in the nation and are well below the national level in areas of achievement, maturity, and ethical thinking. WHY DO YOU CONTINUE LIVING, MRS. MANN? WHY DON'T YOU DO YOURSELF A FAVOR?

ELEANOR. Please leave now.

ELAINE. One more thing, Mrs. Mann. Even though you and your family are going to have to leave tonight before the fuller brush man is scheduled to arrive, he isn't going to come for you anyway. But you'll never know for sure, cause you'll be gone. So long, Mrs. Mann! Enjoy Iceland!

ELEANOR. Wait! How do you know about the fuller brush man? Who are you? He will come! I know it. God has promised that he will come.

ELAINE. So long, you slob! (*Elaine exits.*)

ELEANOR. The Fuller Brush Man will come. I know it. He will come! (*Enter Ronald. Freeze. Exit Eleanor.*)

RONALD. The Nature and Purpose of the Universe. Chapter 10. This particular Tuesday Andy sat in the last row in health class and watched the other boys play with themselves. Andy realized that he would never be able to masturbate. Egged on by the other boys, Andy tried rubbing his sensitive skin, but the stitches popped and he started to bleed. The school nurse gave him a sanitary napkin and took his temperature rectally, in order to humiliate him. Life is going to be difficult for Andy. And all throughout the city of Weehawken, a great search was begun for His Holiness, Pope Paul, and for the assailants of His Holiness' two body guards. (*Exit Ronald. Enter Steve and Fr. Anthony, carrying the limp body of Pope Paul. Elaine, as Sister Annie, follows, carrying a pistol, and shooting behind her.*)

ELAINE. (*Firing.*) Take that, you anti-Christ copper! (*Enter Eleanor.*)

ELEANOR. Steve, what's the matter?

ELAINE. Everybody duck down! (*Everyone drops to the floor except Eleanor.*)

ELEANOR. Steve, who are these people?

ELAINE. I'm the new Pope, and that's the old Pope, and this is Fr. Anthony. (*She fires her gun.*) Pow pow.

ELEANOR. Who is the Pope?

STEVE. Shut up, Eleanor, and make some coffee. (*Enter Andy, bleeding.*)

ANDY. Mommy, Mommy, I've been shot!

ELEANOR. Oh, my God! Steve! Call an ambulance.

ELAINE. What is it? The dirty anti-Christ copper get you, little boy? Huh?

ANDY. I think it came from the house. I got shot in the stomach.

ELEANOR. Oh, Steve! I'll call the hospital.

STEVE. Don't you dare go to that phone!

ELEANOR. But, Steve, we don't know how seriously Andy's been hurt.

STEVE. Look, Eleanor, Sister and I are on a dangerous mission together. If you go to that phone, I'll be forced to kill you.

ELEANOR. Steven. Steven, what's happening?

STEVE. Shut up.

ELAINE. (*Firing.*) Pow pow pow. Pow. Hey, I seem to have run out.

FR. ANT. Are you sure?

ELAINE. I think so. (*She aims her gun at the Pope. The gun goes off, the Pope's body jumps.*) Pow. Oh, my God.

FR. ANT. You've shot the Pope!

ELAINE. The Pretender Pope, you fool. Well, it was meant

to happen. Give me his tiara. (*She puts tiara on her head. Shooting out window.*) Pow pow pow.

ELEANOR. Steven, I think Andy's passed out.

STEVE. Would you shut up? Where's the coffee?

ELAINE. Well, now that the old Pope's dead, we won't have to take him with us tonight.

FR. ANT. Just as well.

ELEANOR. Who are you? Where are you going?

ELAINE. (*To Steve.*) You didn't tell her.

STEVE. She can't be trusted.

ELAINE. She can be trusted under gunpoint. Look here, Mrs. Mann. At exactly midnight tonight the Mystical Body of Christ Kaffe-Klatch Club of Bernardsville is lowering a helicopter into your backyard, and you and your family will have the honor of accompanying me, Sister Annie De Maupassant, the radical nun of Bernardsville and the once and future Pope, as I leave for my exile in Iceland.

ELEANOR. Iceland. Why Iceland?

STEVE. Eleanor, don't ask the Pope questions.

ELAINE. Go ahead. Ask me. I just won't answer.

ELEANOR. She's not the one I'm asking. I'm asking you.

ELAINE. "She" is the cat's mother. I am the Pope.

ELEANOR. Steven, as your wife, I ask you why we have to go to Iceland.

STEVE. You're not my wife. You're a piece of dirt. Now make the coffee.

ELEANOR. I won't go to Iceland! (*Fr. Anthony looks at her kindly.*)

FR. ANT. It would be better for you, Mrs. Mann, if you did go. If you stay here, your husband will go to jail for killing one of the Pope's guards.

STEVE. The hell I will. I'll say my wife did it.

ELAINE. This talk is boring. Tell the tiresome woman to go make coffee before I shoot another one of her children.

STEVE. Eleanor, make coffee before the Pope shoots another one of our children. Then pack our bags and tell Donald and Gary to get ready. We've got to sit tight until midnight. (*Exit Eleanor, dragging Andy behind her. Enter Ronald. Actors freeze but do not exit.*)

RONALD. The Nature and Purpose of the Universe. Chapter 11.

That Tuesday night Eleanor's mind was a shambles of thoughts. She worried that Andy would die, she worried that the police outside the house would kill them all or that maybe the Sister Pope inside the house would kill them all. But most of all she worried that she would not be able to get away at midnight with the Fuller Brush Man. And the strange prophecy of the census lady about going to Iceland came back to haunt her with an uncomfortable persistence. (*Exit Ronald. Enter Donald, Gary. End freeze, action resumes.*)

GARY. (*Seeing the Pope.*) Oh my God. (*Bends down.*) Look at those earrings.

DONALD. God damn. I'll have to start all over again in Iceland. I have my clientele all settled out here in Maplewood and everything. I'm a familiar face. No one wants to have to start up all over again. Especially in Iceland.

STEVE. Donald, we've got to keep the family together at all costs. Isn't that so, Your Holiness?

ELAINE. The family is the essential unit of man. When the family crumbles, society crumbles. When society crumbles, man crumbles. But God never crumbles. (*Starts to shriek in her "speaking in tongues" manner.*)

FR. ANT. Your Holiness, calm yourself. We have a long helicopter flight in front of us. (*Enter Eleanor, weeping into dish towel.*)

ELEANOR. Andy's dead.

ELAINE. Let me see if I can raise him up.

ELEANOR. (*Very angry.*) You stay away from him.

STEVE. Eleanor, don't talk to the Pope that way.

ELEANOR. (*Crying.*) Andy was the only one of my sons who was even remotely kind and gentle.

DONALD. Shut up. Every mother wants an emasculated son. You got your wish, so shut up.

FR. ANT. Perhaps His Holiness should speak on death.

ELAINE. Yes. Yes. I should. (*She stands on a table.*) Death comes to us all, my brothers and sisters in Christ. It comes to the richest of us and to the poorest of us. Our days on this earth are rounded by a little sleep. On the one hand, pre-birth. On the other hand, post-death. It's six of one, half a dozen of another. The world about us is but a valley of tears, full of sorrows for the just and blessings for the unjust. But yet even in the appalling spectacle of

28

death we can see God's face looking down on us. We can see His Great Plan. Like some great spider, God weaves an immense web in which to trap us all and then in a fit of righteous rage he eats us. The Eucharist at last finds its just and fitting revenge. But we must not despair that we do not understand God. Rather must we rejoice in our confusion, for in our ignorance is reflected God's wisdom, in our ugliness His beauty, in our imperfections His perfections. For we are the little people of the earth, and His is the power and the glory, and never the twain shall meet. Hubb-ba, hubba-ba, hubb-ba.

STEVE. Thank you, Your Holiness. (*Elaine steps off table.*)

FR. ANT. Hark. I hear the helicopter now.

STEVE. Are the bags packed, Eleanor?

ELEANOR. Yes.

ELAINE. All right. Get ready to board. Fr. Anthony, I've decided that you must stay behind in the living room and cover us as we fly away.

FR. ANT. But, Your Holiness, I shall be arrested.

ELAINE. Casuistry is not my forte, Fr. Anthony. If you die I shall proclaim you a martyr and wear a red gown. Alright, I'm ready to board. (*They start to exit.*)

STEVE. Eleanor, why aren't you moving?

ELEANOR. Steven, I'm not going. I've packed my bags but not to go to Iceland. At midnight I shall be carried away by a kind man who has seen my pain and who in his pity and love has vowed to take me away from this hell.

STEVE. Eleanor, get into the helicopter.

ELEANOR. Steven, no! I will not go!

STEVE. You are my legal wife. I will need you in Iceland to cook and to sew and to clean and to scrub and to get on your back and fulfill your wifely duty.

ELEANOR. Steven, I will not go. I am going to be rescued! I know it! (*Ronald, D., not visible to the actors, not in the room.*)

RONALD. Eleanor, I'm on my way. Don't fear. I'll save you.

ELEANOR. I hear him now! He's coming!

STEVE. Get into the helicopter!

RONALD. Eleanor, Eleanor!

ELEANOR. I hear him. Come quickly. Save me!

ELAINE. (*Slaps her.*) You stupid woman. You hear nothing. Do you think anyone in the entire world would run off with you?

You are worth nothing. This man is entirely a sick invention of your sick and pathetic mind. You are going to go to Iceland with your husband, as is your duty, and you will suffer through a long succession of tedious days and tedious nights, and you will have no rest because you are not meant to have any rest, and you will not complain because you are doing the will of God. (*Slaps her.*) You are supposed to suffer, you stupid, stupid woman!

ELEANOR. (*Hysterical.*) No!! Help me!

RONALD. Eleanor!

ELAINE. Sons, take your mother forcibly to the helicopter. Knock her unconscious if she gives you any trouble.

ELEANOR. Help me!

DONALD. Shut up, slut! (*Donald and Gary carry Eleanor off-stage.*)

ELAINE. What a thoroughly trivial woman.

FR. ANT. Perhaps you should have shown more charity, Your Holiness.

ELAINE. Charity schmarity. Come on, Mr. Mann. To the helicopter. So long, lackey! (*Elaine and Steve exit. Sound of helicopter. Action freezes, Fr. Anthony and the dead Pope exit. Ronald comes forward.*)

RONALD. The Nature and Purpose of the Universe. Chapter 12. That Tuesday night the police finally got Fr. Anthony Hemmer, and he was tried for the murder of Pope Paul and of little Andy. Fr. Hemmer was sentenced to death, but then the sentence was mitigated to life imprisonment and no rest room facilities. And on that Tuesday night on the helicopter ride to Iceland, Sister Annie De Maupassant, the once and future Pope, mysteriously disappeared midflight, Elaine having more important things to do. The Mann family settled in Iceland, much the same as always except that Eleanor was in a deep depression. Steve, having lost his interest in the new Catholicism, now nurtured an infatuation with the First Lady of the Icelandic Stage, the distinguished Olga Rheinholtenbarkerburkerburr. God assigns Elaine to impersonate Olga in a last effort to finish off Eleanor. (*Ronald exits. Enter Eleanor and Steve. They sit in two chairs. Eleanor hardly moves, just stares off in complete distraction. She appears to hear very little.*)

STEVE. Stop looking like a zombie, for God's sake, Eleanor. My God, you should be counting your blessings. The igloo takes care of itself, our son Gary is engaged to the son of the Prime Minister, and our son Donald has the Prime Minister's daughter pulling in $900 a week. With those sorts of connections, I expect I'll be a big shot in Icelandic politics in a few months. Are you listening, Eleanor? Eleanor? Talking to you is like talking to a mop. So, you see, you should cheer up. Your husband's gonna be quite a big shot. (*We hear the voice of an announcer.*)

ANNOUNCER. Good evening, lady and gentleman. Tonight the Baked Alaska is proud to present that first lady of the Icelandic Stage, Dame Olga Rheinholtenbarkerburkerburr! (*Enter Elaine.*)

ELAINE. (*Bowing graciously.*) Thank you. Thank you. I should like to do a dramatic reading for you. (*She dimples.*)

How do I love thee?

Let me count the ways.

One. Two. Three. Four, five, six . . . Seven. Eight.

STEVE. Hey! Don't forget nasal intercourse!

ELAINE. Oh, yes. Thank you. Nine. Ten, eleven, twelve, thirteen, fourteen, fifteen, sixteen, seventeen . . . and . . . eighteen! And now I should like to give you another reading. It is from "Macbeth" by William Shakespeare.

Tomorrow and tomorrow,

And tomorrow . . . (*Goes blank.*)

And tomorrow, and tomorrow, and tomorrow, and tomorrow, and tomorrow, and tomorrow, and tomorrow . . .

STEVE. A song! Sing us a song! Would you look at her, Eleanor. What a piece she is.

ELAINE. I would like to sing a little song for you that was written for me by a little man in a little black hat with beady little eyes and greedy little thighs. (*Sings, tune is "Tiptoe Through the Tulips."**)

Tiptoe through the tundra,

It's a wundra,

We don't catch a chill,

We tiptoe as we use our free will.

Iceskate round the igloo,

If we dig through,

All the tundra here,

We'll find we will be happy next year.

* See Special Note on copyright page.

31

We'll freeze our knees and our toes,
A sneeze will freeze on our nose,
And we will . . .
Tiptoe through the tundra,
And we'll wundra,
When the world will end,
And Jesus is our very best friend!
Dum-dee-dee-dum-dee-dee-dum, dee-dum!
(*Steve applauds.*)

STEVE. Olga. Come join my table.

ELAINE. (*Crossing to him.*) Oh, Mr. Mann, what a faithful fan you are. What's the matter with your wife?

STEVE. She hasn't made the transition from New Jersey yet.

ELAINE. Oh, I see.

STEVE. Give me a kiss.

ELAINE. Oh, Mr. Mann. Do you think I should? What about your wife?

STEVE. She won't notice. (*They kiss.*) Hey, when am I going to get into your pants?

ELAINE. Oh, Mr. Mann, the things you say! Sometimes I'm surprised out of my little biddle empty-headed mind. But I'll tell you. You aren't ever going to get into my pants because I love my husband. (*Louder, directed at Eleanor.*) Yes, my sweet husband used to be a fuller brush man from New Jersey. But now he's found the love of his life in little iddle me. The Fuller Brush Man loves me.

ELEANOR. (*Stirring.*) What?

ELAINE. Oh, Mrs. Mann. I was just telling your husband how I'm married to an ex-Fuller Brush Man from New Jersey, and how happy I am. Why, here he comes now. You can meet him. (*Enter Ronald. He kisses Elaine.*)

RONALD. Hello, darling. How are you? I caught your act from the back. It was magnificent as usual.

ELAINE. Thank you, dear. I'd like you to meet . . .

ELEANOR. It's you. (*Hysterical.*) Oh, please save me, please save me!

STEVE. (*Shakes her.*) STOP THAT. What sort of display are you making? You're embarrassing me!

ELEANOR. Save me, please. It's not too late!

STEVE. Eleanor!

ELAINE. Mr. Mann, let's leave them alone. My husband is very good at dealing with hysterical women. (*Elaine and Steve step aside. In the next section Ronald acts nonchalant and charming and not outwardly mean.*)

ELEANOR. Please, let me explain why I wasn't there that night. The helicopter had come and . . .

RONALD. There, there, Eleanor, don't be so sentimental . . .

ELEANOR. But if you understood why I wasn't there . . .

RONALD. You weren't there?

ELEANOR. No . . . I . . . but didn't you know?

RONALD. No, silly. I never intended to go back to your house. I just wanted you to buy a brush.

ELEANOR. But you said you saw my suffering, and that you'd take me away.

RONALD. My goodness, you're a silly woman. I say that to all my customers. You're not supposed to believe me.

ELEANOR. Save me!

RONALD. Perhaps you'd like a brush now.

ELEANOR. Save me. Take me away from here! (*Steve and Elaine cross back to the two.*)

RONALD. There's nothing I can do with her. She's just a silly little goose. (*Exit Ronald and Elaine.*)

STEVE. Stop that. (*He throws her to the ground.*) Stop making a spectacle of yourself. (*Enter Gary, Donald, and Ralph.*)

GARY. Hello there, Eleanor. On the ground again? Making a scene?

RALPH. Hello, Mrs. Mann, how are you? Gary and I share the Prime Minister's son now, isn't that nice?

DONALD. Stop whimpering, slut. The Prime Minister says he's willing to give me five dollars if he can urinate in your face, so he's coming over right after dinner.

STEVE. Get up, Eleanor. Time to make dinner. (*The four of them kick her lightly on the ground.*) Come on, Eleanor. Get up. Get up. Get up now. (*Phone rings. Steve answers it.*) Hello? Oh. All right. Why, it's for you, Eleanor. Someone is actually on the telephone for you. (*Enter Elaine, way D. She stares out.*)

ELEANOR. (*In tears.*) Hello? Hello? Hello?

ELAINE. (*Not holding a phone, very serious.*) Hello, Eleanor, this is Elaine speaking. I want you to come over to the slaughter house right away. Do you understand, Eleanor? (*The men exit automatically. Elaine crosses over to Eleanor, helps her to lie on the table. Elaine takes out a knife. Enter Ronald.)*

RONALD. The Nature and Purpose of the Universe. Chapter 13. And God said to Elaine, take now thy charge Eleanor, whom thou lovest, and get thee into the land of Moriah; and offer her there for a burnt offering upon one of the mountains which I will tell thee of.

And Elaine came to the place which God had told her of; and she built an altar there, and laid the wood in order, and bound Eleanor her charge, and laid her upon the altar.

And Elaine stretched forth her hand, and took the knife to slay Eleanor. *(Elaine raises the knife very high and then lowers it quickly towards Eleanor.)*

BUT WAIT! And God said to Elaine, spare this woman's life, for I am merciful. And sing forth my glories and my praise, for I am God of Gods, the Father of his children.

ELAINE & RONALD. *(Sing together; Handel:)*

　　Alleluia! Alleluia! Alleluia!

ELEANOR. Kill me! Please kill me! Kill me!

ELAINE & RONALD.

　　Alleluia! Alleluia! Alleluia!

ELEANOR. I don't want to live. Please kill me. Kill me!

BLACKOUT

ADDENDA

Radio Play Version:

The "radio play" version allows the play to be done with fewer actors. The text is the same; only the staging would be different. The play is set in a radio studio, the actors stand in front of microphones; the violence is done by means of sound effects.

One of the dangers of doing the play this way, however, is that the conceit of Ronald and Elaine as agents of God becomes somewhat muddied (because there's a radio actress playing Elaine who's playing, say, Miss Mansfield).

If you do try the play as a radio play, it is most important to keep the story of Eleanor's suffering the "reason" for the play, and not to let the radio "bits" take over the play. In line with that, the less done with who the people are who are putting on the play, the better.

When the play was done this way at the Direct Theatre, the play began with the following taped announcement:

> Good morning, and welcome to WPAX Sunday Sermon, a series of weekly inspirational stories inspired by the spiritual lives of St. Jude, St. Sebastian, and St. Theresa of Avilla. The following schools will be closed tomorrow due to the death of Mother Charles Magdala, O.S.B.: Our Lady of Perpetual Sorrow School, Rockaway, N.J.; Our Lady of Tears School for Boys, Morristown, N.J.; Union Catholic Girls High School, Scotch Plains, N.J.; and Our Lady of Agonizing Suffering, Camden, N.J.

> Our program will begin after a few short ejaculations: Mary, mother of God, pray for us. God, our saviour and our strength, deliver us. Jesus, Mary, and Joseph, pray for us. Mary, conceived without sin, protect us. Jesus, our hope, deliver us. And now our program.

> Today we are privileged to have with us the St. Dominick Inspirational Society Plays from East Rutherford, N.J. They will be performing for you, live from our studios, a play by Christopher Durang entitled "The Nature and Purpose of the Universe."

Tone and Violence in the Play:

There is a difficult balance needed in the performance of this play: Eleanor's plight must be presented sympathetically so we care about her, and yet her suffering must be sufficiently distanced/or theatricalized (particularly in the first ⅔ of the play) so that we can find it funny.

In line with this, I have never seen Eleanor played by an actress who was the proper age to have grown sons; I'm sure it could be done, with the proper actress; but having a younger woman (20 to 30) play the role also works as a distancing device that may be helpful in presenting the play and, perhaps more importantly, also frees us from worry about the physical demands that the actress playing Eleanor must meet. Common sense and individual taste will have to dictate, but I at least offer that you may be safer casting someone young for Eleanor, and someone the audience can recognize as physically spry so they don't have to worry during the violence.

The violence against Eleanor in the play is a tricky problem; and again common sense and personal taste will have to find what works for each production and group of actors. On the one hand, the violence can't be totally fake or simply too mild, or else we'll never find the humor (particularly in the early scenes) of how *preposterously* awful Eleanor's life is. And on the other hand, if the violence is too convincing or too "specific," the play will turn too ugly. To give an example of the latter problem, there was a production in which Donald punched Eleanor in the stomach, the actress realistically acted loss of breath, etc., and the scene turned too ugly. It may have been all the fault of a too realistic reaction, or it may have been that a man punching a woman in the stomach may be too "specific" an image ever to be funny in this play.

I have found that the violence that seems to work best in the productions I've seen is what I might call (vaguely, I realize) "generalized" violence. For instance, it always seems to work when Donald throws Eleanor to the ground: it's a large, sudden action, Eleanor gets to react in fear and terror, but she doesn't have to act a specific, localized pain. Things like the throwings to the ground, kicks, arm twists, hair pullings, anything that an audience knows can be easily faked and that also don't have particular "pain resonance" for us seem the safest things to try.

With the violence in particular and with the playing tone in general, the problem is somehow to balance letting the audience feel liking and sympathy for Eleanor at the same time that they find the humor in seeing her "get it." Each production has to find its own solutions, so I can offer no sweeping suggestions. But being aware of the problem may be helpful.

To Do the Play in Two Acts:

If you want to place an intermission in the play, you can do so at the end of Chapter 6, with one small addition. At the end of the hymn, after Ronald says "The Nature and Purpose of the Universe. End of Part I.", Eleanor should then say: "Thank God." Then intermission.

Another place to put an intermission is at the end of Chapter 9. If you do that, you should cut Ronald's remarks about Andy at the beginning of Chapter 10, and only leave in his comments about the Pope and the search for the Pope.

PROPERTY LIST

Dish towel
Cereal box
Cereal bowls
Silverware
Coffee cups
(Other breakfast props at director's discretion)
Frying pan
Spatula
Newspaper
Vacuum cleaner
Doll (for "Caroline")
Hypodermic (preferably the trick kind, with the needle on a spring; in
  most novelty stores)
TV
Cigarette, matches (Sister Annie)
Glitter
Papers, rubber bands (Miss Mansfield)
Laundry basket with laundry
Jump rope
Bow (for Andy's hair)
Telephone
Suitcase
Clipboard and pencil ⎫
Roll of film   ⎬ (for Census lady)
Affidavit   ⎭
Guns
Pope's earrings, tiara
Knife (large carving knife)
Scrap of paper (Pope)
Photos, in purse (Elaine)
Tiara (Elaine)

DEATH COMES TO US ALL, MARY AGNES

DEATH COMES TO US ALL, MARY AGNES was first presented at the Yale School of Drama on April 22, 1975, directed by Robert Lewis. The cast was as follows:

MARTIN, a butler .... Ben Halley, Jr.
MARGARET, a maid .... Denise A. Gordon
CORAL TYNE .... Joyce Fideor
HERBERT POMME .... Jeremy Smith
MARGOT POMME, his daughter .... Christine Estabrook
MRS. JANSEN-HUBBELL, her grandmother .... Marcell Rosenblatt
VIVIEN JANSEN-HUBBELL POMME .... Martha Gaylord
TOD POMME, her son .... Alan Mokler
TIM POMME, her son .... Brian McEleney
A & P DELIVERY BOY .... John L. Weil
MARY AGNES SIMPSON, Martin's niece .... Bever-Leigh Banfield
GRAND UNION DELIVERY BOY .... Mark Boyer

SETTING

The set is a Victorian drawing room; if it looks as if "The Mouse-trap" is about to play there, that would be the right idea. There should be a comfortable, expensive sofa; an arm chair or two; an old coffee table; probably an Oriental rug. There should be an entrance to the house u. l.; there might also be a staircase leading to upstairs, also u. l. The entranceway, or right below it, should have an old telephone and telephone stand. There should be exits, r. and l., one to servants quarters, the other to other rooms in the downstairs area.

The two non-drawing room scenes (Vivien's bedroom, and the grandmother locked up in the Tower) should be differentiated mostly by lighting; a change of set would be time-consuming and laborious. Vivien's bedroom should be d. r. in a small spotlight, with a pink boudoir chair brought in as the only piece of furniture; for the second scene set in the bedroom, a milk carton (or some particularly ratty chair) should be brought in by the maid for the grandmother to sit on. And then the brief scene in the "Tower" should be performed d. l., with the same milk carton or chair and maybe one or two dead rats, in a small spotlight.

(Note: if you have a particularly wide stage, you could consider leaving small sets for the bedroom and the Tower onstage, l. and r., for the whole play; if you left them unlit when they were not in use, presumably they would not then be distracting.) Note on the characters of Tod and Tim: in the casting and playing of these roles, it would be a good idea to avoid effeminacy or other cliches often found in the theatrical presentation of homosexuals. I prefer that they either appear as well mannered and well dressed, rather like models from "Gentlemen's Quarterly," or else, a somewhat more bizarre choice, as very "regular guys" (sort of like casting Paul Newman and Steve McQueen in the roles, when they were in their 20s).

SCENE 1

The setting is a Victorian drawing room in East Haddam, Vermont, Couch, chairs, etc. An oriental rug. A telephone on a telephone stand. After a few beats, the phone rings. Enter Margaret, a maid, about 50 years old.

MARGARET. Hello, Mr. Jansen-Hubbell's residence, East Haddam, Vermont, the scullery maid speaking. No, I'm sorry, Mr. Jansen-Hubbell cannot come to the phone. He is upstairs dying, Lord have mercy on his soul, and cannot be disturbed. Can I take a message? Yes, you *could* speak to Mrs. Jansen-Hubbell, if you like, but she's mad as a hatter, poor dear, and as liable to clip herself to death with scissors as not. Why don't you just give me the message? I am a trusted and beloved servant of many years distinguished service. I first came to work for Mr. Jansen-Hubbell in early May of 1942, during the war. It was a terrible war, it was, I had just come over from England on ship, it was a stormy and . . . (*Enter Coral Tyne, age 33 or so, elegant, mean. She is dressed in a man's suit, tie, etc.*)
CORAL. Margaret, go back to the scullery please. I've told you to keep to the kitchen, and that Martin takes care of the living quarters.
MARGARET. (*Nasty.*) Well, I don't see that he answered the phone, did he? The way you treat Martin with such kow-towin' and praise, you'd think he was the King of England or something . . .
CORAL. Don't waste my time with your petty complaints. Just give me the phone and withdraw to the lower recesses of the house please.
MARGARET. You can go straight to hell, Missy. (*Exits.*)

CORAL. (*Into phone.*) Hello. This is Coral Tyne speaking, Mr. Jansen-Hubbell's secretary. May I help you? What? You make what? Speak up. Light bulbs? Why are you calling me, selling light bulbs? Because you're what? Try to enunciate please. Hand what? Oh. Handicapped. Oh, I see. Well, I'm sorry, I'm not in-' terested. You should sell your light bulbs to someone else. Stop stuttering. Goodbye. (*Hangs up. Enter Martin, the butler, distinguished, older.*)

MARTIN. Miss Tyne, perhaps you should prepare Mrs. Jansen-Hubbell. Her son-in-law and granddaughter have just arrived.

CORAL. If you mean Herbert and Margot, why don't you say Herbert and Margot? Drop the formality, for God's sake.

MARTIN. I have never understood why Mr. Jansen-Hubbell allows you to be so rude to me. (*Coral exits. Enter Herbert Pomme, age 58, all gray, smallish man, quiet, missing one arm, his jacket sleeve hanging loosely. With him is his daughter Margot, age 24, dressed drably, hair pulled back, unhappy, manic.*)

MARGOT. Oh, Daddy, look—the mansion's the same as it always was.

HERBERT. So few things change.

MARGOT. And there's Martin.

MARTIN. Hello, Miss Margot. Mr. Pomme.

HERBERT. Martin.

MARGOT. You look much older, Martin. How is Grandad? Is he very bad?

MARTIN. Yes. He awaits death. He refuses his morning juice. His chronic wince worsens.

MARGOT. Does Grandma know what's going on?

MARTIN. Mrs. Jansen-Hubbell has feigned madness so long that she barely has to feign it any more.

MARGOT. (*Upset.*) Grandad hasn't been keeping her in the Tower again, has he?

HERBERT. You mustn't fight it, angel.

MARGOT. Grandad has such a cruel streak in him. It must be where my mother gets her meanness from. (*To Martin.*) Oh, please send for Grandma from the Tower.

MARTIN. I've already done so, Miss Margot.

HERBERT. Has Vivien arrived yet?

MARTIN. Not yet, Mr. Pomme.

HERBERT. I don't much look forward to seeing my wife again after all these years.

MARGOT. She's your ex-wife. Just as she's my ex-mother. (*Enter Coral and Mrs. Jansen-Hubbell. Mrs. Jansen-Hubbell is 68, dressed in black, her hands are bound together at the wrists, her eyes are wild and deeply circled. As she enters she spits out butterscotch pudding all over the stage.*) Grandma! What's the matter?

CORAL. (*Calling off-stage.*) Margaret! (*Holding a dead rat.*) I found her chewing on this when I went up there! (*To Mrs. J-H, meanly.*) I've told you you'll make yourself sick! (*Waves dead rat in Mrs. J-H's face.*)

MARGOT. Miss Tyne, please. (*Enter Margaret.*)

MARGARET. What do you want? Oh, it's Miss Margot. Are your two handsome brothers here yet?

MARGOT. No, they're not! (*Hysterical.*) Oh, why does everyone always favor my brothers over me? They were always the pretty ones, the ones who were excused when they were bad, the one who were loved! I want love!

HERBERT. Margot, please. Control yourself.

MARGOT. (*Whimpering.*) I'm sorry, Father. It must be the strain of grandfather's oncoming death.

CORAL. Margaret, Mrs. Jansen-Hubbell has spit something up on the floor. Wipe it up, will you please?

MARGARET. May your soul rot in hell and the devils cause you unspeakable torment. (*She wipes up mess.*)

CORAL. There is no hell, Margaret. (*To others.*) I shall leave you to your memories. Martin, please remove the rat. (*Martin and Coral exit. Margaret exits as soon as she's finished cleaning up.*)

MARGOT. (*Bringing Mrs. Jansen-Hubbell to sofa.*) Grandma, do you remember me? It's your little Margot. Sit down, let me look at you. Do you remember me? I remember you, way back before you first feigned madness. Do you remember that summer I was fifteen, and Daddy and I came to visit right after he'd found the French orphanage my mother had put me in? And Grandad had just got the first of his secretaries. Remember? It was Miss Willis, then, I think. And I asked you why Mama had put me in an orphanage like I didn't belong to her, just so she could go to Italy with her two boys, her two sons, my twin brothers! She left me there for five years! (*Getting teary and hysterical.*) And I said to you, Grandma, will there ever be anyone in this world who will love me? Love *me* for what I am, and love me and not pity

43

me? And you looked at me and you said, "No," and I said, "But Grandma, Why?" And you said, "Because there never was for me!" Do you remember, Grandma? There never was for me! (*She weeps hysterically, Mrs. Jansen-Hubbell wails and wails, raising her tied hands up and down in rhythm.*)

HERBERT. Margot, please! These memories do us no good. Margot. (*Enter Coral with a large gong, which she strikes three times.*)

CORAL. May I remind you that we have a dying man in this house. We must have quiet. (*Enter Martin.*)

MARTIN. Mr. Pomme, your ex-wife has just arrived. If you wished to avoid seeing her right away, might I suggest retiring to your room?

HERBERT. Yes. I think I might take a nap. It's been a hard trip, eh, Margot?

MARGOT. Father, you've got to face her. Don't be afraid. I'll help you.

HERBERT. There's plenty of time, Margot. I need a hot bath. (*He exits quickly.*)

MARGOT. Oh, why is he so weak?

MARTIN. Human nature, my child.

MARGOT. Mind your place, Martin. (*Enter Margaret.*)

MARGARET. They're coming! I saw them. The boys are here. And as handsome as the day I saw them last. More so.

CORAL. Get back to the scullery.

MARGARET. May eagles of the Lord tear out your heart and scatter it to the winds. (*Enter Vivien Jansen-Hubbell Pomme, flanked on either side by her sons Tod and Tim. Vivien is 45, attractive, dressed expensively. She can't walk very well, she has no feeling in her legs and can walk only with support from others. She is usually supported by her sons. Tod and Tim are 26, fraternal twins, looks quite similar. They wear expensive suits, and generally look like an ad from "Gentlemen's Quarterly.")*

VIVIEN. I've returned! (*Pause.*) How nice. The servants have gathered to greet us.

MARGARET. You look wonderful, ma'am.

VIVIEN. Thank you, Margaret.

MARTIN. Superb, madame.

VIVIEN. Do I really?

MARTIN. You do indeed.

CORAL. Mr. Jansen-Hubbell has expected you.

VIVIEN. One always wants one's children at one's death bed.

MARGARET. The boys look wonderful too, ma'am. As handsome as their mother is beautiful.

VIVIEN. Thank you, dear. It's the Mediterranean sun, I expect. Men always look better tanned.

MARGOT. Hello, Mother.

VIVIEN. You must be a new maid of Father's?

MARGOT. I called you "Mother."

VIVIEN. Did you? Well, I can't be expected to listen to every word people say to me. Children, help me sit down. (*Tod and Tim help her to a chair, then stand by her.*)

MARGOT. I'm your daughter, Mother. How do you think I look?

VIVIEN. I gave my daughter to a French orphanage many years ago. It was an act of kindness because I realized I had not the temperament to raise girls—as I did have the temperament to raise boys, my two fine boys, my twin stars. I expect the girl's still there, unless she drowned at sea or died in a car accident. As for your personal appearance, whoever you are, it is drab and depressing. Your entire demeanour is singularly unpleasant. The world is far too drab and depressing as it is; one should try to glitter to make up for it. But I've spent too much time discussing appearance with a complete stranger, and I've ignored my mad mother. How are you, Mother? (*Martin brings Mrs. Jansen-Hubbell closer to Vivien.*) Do you have any lucid moments these days, or is it all mist and haze? Oh, you've dribbled something on your nice mourning frock. That shouldn't be. Miss Tyne, does Father know that mother is out of the Tower?

CORAL. Your father is dying, Mrs. Pomme.

VIVIEN. That was not the question. The question was why is my mother not up in the Tower where it doesn't matter if she dribbles over the sofa and the carpets? And I am not to be called Mrs. Pomme. I refer to myself by my maiden name of Jansen-Hubbell, a name you are quite familiar with, I am sure, Miss Tyne. After all, you've been under my father for many years now. (*Silence.*) His service, I mean.

CORAL. Your father wished you to greet your mother before I placed her back in the Tower.

VIVIEN. I think I've greeted her long enough. Haven't I, mother? You're not going to be lucid, are you? (*No response.*) There,

45

you see. Take her away, Miss Tyne. And Martin, you might run my bath. My legs always ache at this time of day. And Margaret, you might bring the boys some tea and graham crackers, you remember how fond Tod and Tim are of graham crackers.

MARGARET. Indeed, I do, Ma'am. (*She and Martin exit.*)

VIVIEN. And, Miss Tyne, would you relate to my Father my wishes for his continued health, and that I shall see him after I take my bath.

CORAL. Yes, Miss Jansen-Hubbell.

VIVIEN. *Mrs.* Jansen-Hubbell, *Miss* Tyne. I have two sons, you are aware.

CORAL. Yes, Mrs. Jansen-Hubbell. (*Exits with grandmother. Tod and Tim sit on couch together.*)

VIVIEN. Well, children, I expect once the will is revealed, we'll be able to count on a good many more summers in Italy together.

MARGOT. Maybe he'll leave all his money to me.

VIVIEN. Children, do you hear an additional voice? (*Tod and Tim grin at one another, enjoying the joke.*) I hope I'm not losing my grasp like my poor lamented mother.

TOD. I'm sure you're perfectly sane, Mother.

VIVIEN. Before I take my bath, we can have a nice talk about art and literature.

MARGOT. Mother, someday you will be punished.

VIVIEN. Tell me, Tod, about your new idea for a play. And Tim, why don't you sketch me. Mother listening to her sons. (*Tim sketches.*)

TOD. I thought of it the other day when Tim and I were sunbathing. The play would deal with a society where women were completely outlawed, except for a few captives who were allowed to have male off-spring. They'd be impregnated by artificial insemination. And so all the women would be cut off and separated from the male society, because they were the cause of evil, all except for one woman who was worshipped by the men as a goddess.

TIM. You can pose for the goddess, Mother. We could do it in oils.

TOD. And all the men worship this woman-goddess, and then in the evenings when all the men retire to their various chambers, the woman-goddess would cry herself to sleep because none of the men will touch her.

VIVIEN. What would the ending be?

TOD. I haven't one yet.

TIM. A bolt of lightning could kill everybody.

VIVIEN. It's not one of my favorite ones. I prefer the one about the wonderful Princess who has to choose between two beautiful Princes and she can't make up her mind and so she runs off with both of them and lives happily ever after.

TOD. I never wrote that.

VIVIEN. I know. I just did, and I love it. (*Enter Martin.*)

MARTIN. Your bath is ready, madam.

VIVIEN. Thank you, Martin. Children, you stay here for tea. Martin will help me to my room. (*Martin helps Vivien hobble off.*)

MARGOT. For a second, I thought I was included in the "children."

TIM. Isn't it time you outgrew these petty jealousies, Margot?

MARGOT. Oh, so I'm actually going to get talked to, am I?

TOD. It's only Mama who's good at games. We're much more direct.

TIM. (*To Tod.*) I'm bored already. Do you want to play pot luck?

TOD. Why not? There's the phone.

TIM. (*Dials.*) Could I have the number of the A & P please?

MARGOT. That's domestic.

TOD. Just a game we play. (*Tim dials again.*)

MARGOT. It's pretty good to be 26 and still be making prank phone calls.

TOD. There's no need to wallow in maturity.

TIM. Hello. Would you send a delivery boy out to the Jansen-Hubbell residence on Crestview Street? Just assorted groceries will do. As much as you like. Thank you. Oh, and tell him to use the front door. Yes, thank you.

MARGOT. It seems a worthless joke to charge things to grandfather. He can certainly afford it, but after all he *is* dying.

TOD. So are we all, Sis.

TIM. So how's life been since we saw you last. Did you like the orphanage?

TOD. You've grown up passably pretty, I see.

MARGOT. Not as pretty as you two, I'm sure.

TOD. Beauty, Margot, is in the eye of the beholder. If most beholders don't take to you, don't blame us.

TIM. It's probably your glum and depressing demeanor.

MARGOT. Why shouldn't I be glum? I spent the early part of my childhood in some horrible institution while mother told father I was with her travelling the continent. Getting rid of me was like drowning a kitten to her.

TIM. You rather look like a drowned kitten.

TOD. Too big. Cat.

MARGOT. I've read Freud. I know what psychological damage has been done to me. People shouldn't be allowed to have children until they've passed a test in psychology. Anyone who gets below B minus should be sterilized. My mother should be the one locked up in the Tower, not Grandma . . .

TOD. God'll strike you dead if you talk that way.

MARGOT. God won't, but Mama sure as hell will.

TIM. Look, Margot, you're a very neurotic girl, and you have some biological claim to be our sister, and we wish we could help you . . .

TOD. But we can't think of a gosh-darned thing to say, so maybe you should go off and complain to your poor, silly father. If you're here, I presume he can't be far away.

MARGOT. I never dreamed such wickedness existed. (*Exits.*)

TOD. To describe the everyday procedure of breathing, eating, and sleeping as wickedness bespeaks a parochial outlook and an alarming failure to grasp reality.

TIM. Hear, hear. (*Enter Margaret with tea and graham crackers.*)

MARGARET. Ah, and here's tea for my two handsome boys.

TIM. Ah, and here's Margaret, and God love her too.

TOD. We've missed you, Margaret. We've had many a wet dream over you.

MARGARET. Master Tod, what can you be thinking of?

TIM. You, Margaret, and can you blame us?

TOD. Ah, the Lord bless you, Maggie.

TIM. Better be off with you now (*He pats her rear.*) lest we can control ourselves no longer.

MARGARET. Oh Master Tim! Are you flirting with me now?

TOD. Well, knowing Tim, you better not stick around to find out.

MARGARET. Oh, the Lord up in heaven, if this isn't a day. (*She exits cheerily.*)

TIM. She's more like a cow than I remembered. (*Door bell.*) Oh, is it pot luck already?

TOD. I bet it is. Blond or dark?

TIM. Blond.

TOD. All right, if it's a blond, it's yours. (*Enter Martin.*) Oh, we'll get it, Martin. We're expecting someone.

MARTIN. Very well. (*Exits. Tim goes to door, ushers in blond grocery boy about 16, carrying several packages and wearing thick glasses.*)

TIM. Ah, you've come at last.

TOD. Blond, but not too terrific. But then that's pot luck.

TIM. We haven't eaten since last Tuesday. What have you brought us?

BOY. I don't know. The manager packed it.

TOD. How clever.

BOY. Will that be cash or charge?

TIM. Charge, of course.

BOY. (*Taking out slip.*) Well, I'll just fill this out.

TIM. (*Hand on boy's shoulder.*) What's the hurry? Here, sit down. (*He forces boy to sit on couch between them.*) We can talk about life.

BOY. I have to get right back.

TIM. (*Pushing him back.*) Relax.

TOD. (*To boy, accent perhaps.*) You want to buy my sister? She is a virgin.

TIM. (*Laughs.*) Hey, you know, that might even be true.

BOY. Just let me fill out the charge form . . .

TIM. (*Snatching off boy's glasses.*) Hey calm down.

BOY. Wait. I can hardly see without my glasses. (*Boy's eyes are not focused.*)

TIM. (*Looking right at boy.*) Young . . . young . . . young man. Perhaps you will see better without your glasses.

BOY. What?

TIM. You want to stay with us tonight? We all have a good time. Everybody needs a little friendship. (*Arm on shoulder again.*)

BOY. Let me go.

TOD. (*Dropping the playfulness.*) If not friendship, money then. Hey, boy, look at me. (*Boy tries to.*) Would you like to make some money? Do you understand me? (*Slow.*) We . . . will . . . pay . . . you.

BOY. I can't see your expression clearly. If this is a joke, I can't tell.

TIM. Oh throw him back in the bay. He's too small. Here are your glasses. (*Boy leaves in a hurry.*) Don't call us, we'll call you.

TOD. Obvious latent homosexual. Did you see the way he bolted from the room?

TIM. I suspect he had acne on his back. (*Goes to phone, dials.*) Could I have the number of the Grand Union please?

BLACKOUT

SCENE 2

Vivien's bedroom. No real change of set. Just spot Vivien in bathrobe, towel around her head, she's just taken her bath. She's seated, speaking into microphone.

VIVIEN. Dear Diary, I have just finished taking my bath and have hobbled to this chair. Sometimes I think that the growing weakness in my legs, this creeping paralysis, is God's judgment on me. But I won't accept that. I refuse to be judged. And I will enjoy this last part of my life, I will. I hated the first twenty years, my father was such an unpleasant man. Father is dying, by the way, and good riddance. I hope I get most of the money.

New paragraph. I had the hiccups in the car on the way up here. Tod and Tim were very helpful. We tried holding my breath, and we tried tickling me. Then we had a car accident, and they went away.

New paragraph. With great beauty comes responsibility—to look lovely, to be charming, to wear clothes well. I feel I have met this responsibility all my life, and so have my wonderful sons Tod and Tim. I bought Tod and Tim matching olive swim trunks today, and watched them swim. I wore a sweet and rather enormous caftan, $750, Nieman Marcus. Tod said I looked rather like a circus tent, but I feel he was being witty rather than nasty. Ah, how transitory is beauty. Perhaps that should be a new paragraph.

New paragraph. Ah, how transitory is beauty. Here today, gone 40 years later, perhaps, in my case, 50. Tod and Tim exercise constantly in front of mirrors. I have always loved mirrors because they tell the truth, and I am a great believer in the truth, at least in terms of my own physical beauty. I was the most beautiful young girl who ever lived. I hope you will not think this is mere hyperbole: I have made a list of the various men and women who have expressed ecstasy at my beauty over the past many years, and on request I will give the names and addresses of those people, a list that runs on for 300 pages, single spaced, both sides. Dr. and Mrs. Francis Wallaby, Hampshire Castle, England; the Reverend Edgar Lancaster of St. Gertrude-by-the-Tarn Church of the Martyrs, Melody Brook, New Hampshire; Dr. Harold Metterly, New York City, who treated me for a social disease in 1947. The list goes on and on. Swami Rim Krishna. Wallace Bartholomew and his mother Dame Alice Bartholomew. That drunken Irishman named Bucky or Biffy or something. Many, many people.

New paragraph. Sometimes in the early mornings I feel a sadness. I know that later in the day I will go to the hairdresser, or visit my dying father, or watch Tod and Tim swim. But nowhere in my day do I experience a kind thought or a shared response or even just a simple gesture of relaxation. And I quietly mourn the fact that I have been cast to play the role I play, that I can't be someone more elevated, more hopeful, even just more human. However, I suppose one can't have everything. I am very beautiful and charming, and everyone likes me. And I should be glad I'm not a blind person or an Avon representative or just someone who works as a clerk in an insurance company and who dies at the age of 63. And so I stare out sometimes in the morning and relish my fleeting sadness, and then I begin the day.

New paragraph. I fear that God won't think I've been a good mother. I fear that his criteria of judgment will be limited, old-fashioned. I fear I will be punished. I fear I will be punished.

BLACKOUT

SCENE 3

The drawing room. Herbert sits reading, a standing lamp by his side. Enter Margaret; she sits and begins scouring pots she has brought with her.

HERBERT. Margaret, please. Why aren't you in the kitchen?
MARGARET. There are all those goddamned boy scouts in the

kitchen. Mr. Jansen-Hubbell refuses to see them, and they say they won't leave until they give him some plaque or other.

HERBERT. I don't know anything about it. (*Tries to read.*)

MARGARET. I never saw the point in being a boy scout. (*She scrubs.*)

HERBERT. Margaret, please, I'm reading. (*Enter Margot.*)

MARGOT. Oh, Father, there you are. I've got to talk to someone.

HERBERT. Margot, it's been a tiring day. I'm reading.

MARGARET. Oh, God, another scene. You're a very unbalanced girl. I've never liked you, but to be fair I guess it must be hard to have to live up to two such wonderful people as your brothers.

MARGOT. Why do you insist on thinking of them as wonderful. Those two fags!

MARGARET. That's a nasty thing to say. You probably only accuse them of that because you fear it in yourself. (*To Herbert.*) Isn't that so?

MARGOT. Margaret, leave the study at once.

MARGARET. I don't see that you have no boy friend. Unless you want to count your father. (*Exits.*)

MARGOT. Go to hell.

HERBERT. Margot, please. Your mother will hear the shouting and come down.

MARGOT. That would be fine. It's time someone told her off. Oh, Father, stop reading. (*She turns off his light.*) I feel so upset seeing Mother and my brothers again, after all these years. I've hated them in the abstract for so long that it's almost disappointing not to find them superhumanly hateful. (*He turns on the light, she turns it off.*) Will you stop that? Last night I had that awful dream again.

HERBERT. Margot, you work yourself up over nothing. Lots of girls dream they're Joan of Arc.

MARGOT. (*Angry.*) I don't mean the Joan of Arc dream. This is the one where I'm in the orphanage and I see my mother in a field with my two brothers, canoeing. And rather than feeling angry at her for putting me in the orphanage, I just feel this terrible longing to be accepted by them, by her. And then I find that I'm dressed like a boy and that I've even grown a moustache, and I go out to them to show my mother that I'm a boy and then I notice that I'm still wearing lip stick, and I try to wipe it off but there's so much of it I can't get it off, and I keep wiping it and wiping it, and the three of them just laugh and laugh at me, and then they steer their canoe at me and it comes racing towards me to crush me, and a great big oar from the canoe hits me on top of the head, and then the oar starts to beat me repeatedly, ecstatically. And then I wake up. Trembling.

HERBERT. What do you want me to say? The oar's a phallic symbol. You should stay away from boating. Don't grow a moustache.

MARGOT. (*Takes his book, throws it across the room.*) I feel such anger and unhappiness all the time! When you rescued me from the orphanage, I thought I was finally saved and that things would be all right. But they weren't. You don't hate mother. And you don't like me. What am I to do? I've been seeing my psychiatrist for three years now, four times a week, and I don't feel any change. I feel such a prisoner to my past. And I have such a longing for normality. I see people on the street who eat in cafeterias and have families and go to parks and who aren't burdened with this terrible bitterness; and I want to be like them. So much I want to be like them.

HERBERT. No one's going to like you if you throw books, Margot.

MARGOT. That has nothing to do with it. I don't think you've been even listening . . . (*Enter Mary Agnes, 19, carrying pocket book, has coat on.*)

MARY AGNES. (*To Herbert.*) How do you do? You must have come about my little dog.

MARGOT. Who are you?

MARY AGNES. You must be Margot. I'm Martin's niece, Mary Agnes Simpson. (*Back to Herbert.*) There's been a terrible accident, Doctor. My little dog has been cut into pieces. The pieces are on the bed. My husband says that roving bands of little boys did it, but I don't believe it. I think my husband did it.

MARGOT. What are you talking about?

MARY AGNES. You're probably too sweet to understand. (*To Herbert.*) You see, my husband did it as a cruelty to me. I mean the sight was quite horrible. The dog's eyes were gouged out—I found one eye in my bathroom glass, Lord knows where I'll find the other one—its stomach was slit open and its innards were mixed with some of my cancelled checks. It's peculiar. I didn't even cry out, I just said, My husband has done this. (*Smiles.*)

53

We're very eccentric, you see. (*To Margot.*) Margot, dear, when Martin comes down, tell him I want to see him in his room. (*Starts to exit, turns to Herbert.*) Oh, yes. Thank you for coming. (*Starts to exit again.*)

MARGOT. Wait. Does Martin know you're here? (*Touches her arm.*)

MARY AGNES. (*Violent.*) Don't clutch at me! Don't you clutch at me. I will not be clutched at! (*She has an epileptic fit on the ground. Herbert stands on chair to get out of way.*)

MARGOT. Oh my God. What's the matter? Help! (*Margaret and Martin rush in.*)

MARTIN. What's she doing here?

MARGARET. If it's not one thing, it's another.

MARGOT. What shall we do?

MARTIN. Just wait. It'll pass. (*There is silence as all watch Mary Agnes thrash about on the floor. Then she subsides. Martin helps her up.*)

MARTIN. Aren't you ashamed? A girl your age. We're going to have to keep a closer watch on you.

MARY AGNES. Oh, Uncle Martin, Skippy is dead. He's dead. My puppy is gone.

MARTIN: He's gone to puppy heaven. We have to face these tragedies in life, Mary Agnes, and believe that even though things seem terrible, they aren't really. Why, if I believed that things were the way they seemed, I couldn't go on for more than a day. Now, do you feel better, dear?

MARY AGNES. Yes, Uncle.

MARTIN. How did you get here?

MARY AGNES. I have my volkswagon outside.

MARTIN. Alright. Now why don't you go get in it, and go back to your husband. I bet he's worried about you. Here, Margaret will help you to the car.

MARY AGNES. He shouldn't have killed the puppy.

MARTIN. It was probably an accident. Now, go on along.

MARY AGNES. Can't I stay with you tonight?

MARTIN. No, dear. Your husband will miss you.

MARY AGNES. All right. (*Suddenly very cheerful.*) Goodbye, everybody. (*She and Margaret exit.*)

MARTIN. (*To Herbert.*) She's just newly married and is having some trouble adjusting.

HERBERT. I think you handled it very well, Martin.

MARTIN. Thank you. One learns to cope. (*He exits.*)

HERBERT. I didn't know Martin had a niece.

MARGOT. Father, I want you to go right up to her and tell her you hate her.

HERBERT. Who? His niece?

MARGOT. No. My mother. Tell her just so she knows.

HERBERT. She knows already.

MARGOT. Then why are you afraid to tell her?

HERBERT. Margot, you're spoiling my evening. I can't read, the boy scouts are here, and we're plagued with epileptics. Why can't we be civilized?

MARGOT. She's the one who's not civilized! This is the woman who's maimed me. I'm psychologically maimed.

HERBERT. You seem fine to me, dear.

MARGOT. Well, you don't see very well, do you? (*Enter Coral, shaken.*)

CORAL. Oh, there you are. I wonder if I might see you for a moment.

HERBERT. I'll leave.

CORAL. No, I want to speak to both of you. I've just spoken to Mr. Jansen-Hubbell. He was in a wretched mood after all those boy scouts, and he told me that he plans to reveal his will tomorrow and that . . . he intends to leave all his money to Mrs. Pomme— that is, to Vivien, or Mrs. Jansen-Hubbell, or whatever she's being called.

MARGOT. He has so much money, surely he's leaving all of us something.

CORAL. No, he says, he plans to show the injustice of the world through his will and leave it all to that awful woman. And I feel so . . . so awful. (*She begins to cry, deep sobs.*)

HERBERT. Excuse me. (*Exits.*)

CORAL. I've worked for your grandfather for 12 years. When he first hired me, I slept with him only because I thought he'd eventually leave me some of his money. Not all of it, just some. It was so degrading. I don't like men much anyway, and your grandfather's mouth tasted like a septic tank. But I put up with his demands and perversions. He used to pour egg yolks on me and lick them off. I was disgusted. Egg yolks. I just kept thinking through it all, someday it will pay off, someday I'll be rich, and then my years of bitterness will be answered. And now I find he's planning to die and he has no plans for me at all. None at all. I could have married a druggist back in Hightstown if it hadn't been for your grandfather. Oh, what am I going to do?

MARGOT. (*Surprised.*) Miss Tyne, you're asking for sympathy for your own greed. People are responsible for their own actions, Miss Tyne. You can't blame my grandfather that you didn't marry a druggist. Money is so unimportant, Miss Tyne. It is love and affection, that matters. Comfort yourself with that thought. (*Exits. Coral cries.*)

BLACKOUT

SCENE 4

Vivien's bedroom. Dressed in fancy negligee.

VIVIEN. (*Seated, calling off-stage.*) Tod? Tim? Are you asleep already? Tod? Tim? Are you there? Oh, dear. Oh, my. Such a long night ahead of me. (*Enter Margaret with Mrs. Jansen-Hubbell, whose hands are bound per usual.*) Oh, Margaret, you've brought Mother! Thank goodness!

MARGARET. Just thought you could say good night to your dear mother. She needs an outing.

VIVIEN. O precious Mother. Sit down. Both of you. Oh, I'm so glad you've come. Tod and Tim have already gone to bed and I've no one to talk to, and I'm so lonely.

MARGARET. Well, your mother's here to comfort you.

VIVIEN. Is she? (*Clutching her mother.*) Are you, Mother? Are you going to be lucid, Mother, and touch my hair and say, "Vivien, my daughter"? (*Pause.*) Well, I thought not. Oh, Mother, do you think Tod and Tim love me enough, do you?

MARGARET. (*Answering for Mrs. J-H.*) I'm sure they do. They love their mother.

VIVIEN. (*Looking at her mother as if she had been the one to answer.*) But do they love me enough, that's what I wonder. Oh, it reminds me of my first child, Narcissus.

MARGARET. I don't remember your having another child.

VIVIEN. (*To her mother.*) Of course, you don't, Mother, you're addled.

MARGARET. No, I mean, *I* don't remember your having another child.

VIVIEN. Oh, but I did, Margaret. You can never know. My son Narcissus was the most beautiful boy I have ever seen in my life. More beautiful than Tod and Tim even, though I'd never tell them that. His father was the North Wind and the Gulf Stream, and his skin was like pure alabaster and his hair was black like ravens' feathers gone to heaven. He was my wonderful child. And every morning, I'd wake my little boy with kisses and I'd say, who's the most wonderful son of the most wonderful mother in the world? And the answer would be Narcissus and Vivien. And I remember one day, he came home from nursery school and all his jealous playmates followed angrily behind him, envious of his alabaster skin and raven black hair. The children chanted at him cruelly: "Narcissus is a sissy, Narcissus is a sissy." And I went out into our little backyard and I balanced Narcissus on my shoulders and I said, "Narcissus is the most wonderful son in the world, and Vivien is the most wonderful mother." We spoke of ourselves in the third person a lot in those days. (*Pause.*) Are you listening, Mother?

MARGARET. Yes, dear, I am.

VIVIEN. But then one day, quite suddenly, Narcissus stopped responding fully—he'd beam at my compliments to him, but he wouldn't return them. And one day down in the basement doing our laundry, we played our poem game that went: "Tyger, tyger, burning bright; in the forests of the night; who's the fairest in the land?" And the answer was always Narcissus and Vivien, Vivien and Narcissus. But one day, that one day, Narcissus said, "The answer is me. Narcissus. Not Vivien. Just me." Well . . . it is intolerable not to have your love returned in kind, your love should reflect right off another person and engulf you in a warm, glorious glow of light and love. But Narcissus didn't love me any more. So I picked up a wrench and I hit him over the head, my child; and then I wrapped his once beautiful body in newspapers and I threw him out in the garbage. In the garbage, you understand? Because we all need love, you see. Sigmund used to say to me, "Vivien, you're a peculiar woman and I don't like you much, but at least you don't repress your drives. And you deserve love." Ah, Sigmund. He wrote such beautiful waltzes. He was wrong, of course, I do repress my drives, some of them, but I do deserve love. And I need it. Oh, Mother, do you love me? Do you love me really?

MARGARET. Of course I do. You're my daughter.

VIVIEN. Oh what an ingenuous response. You're my daughter—as if that were enough to insure love. You've a sweet, uncluttered mind, Mother. Thank you for visiting me tonight in my sorrow. (*She kisses her mother.*) Margaret, you can take Mother to the Tower now. I think I'll be able to sleep.

MARGARET. Yes, Mrs. Jansen-Hubbell. Sweet dreams. Come on, dearie. (*Margaret and Mrs. Jansen-Hubbell exit.*)

VIVIEN. (*Reciting softly to herself.*) Dear Diary, I fear I am not loved enough. I fear it. (*Calling.*) Tod? Tim? Are you there? Are you there? (*Listens.*)

BLACKOUT

Scene 5

Drawing room of the mansion again. Enter Martin.

MARTIN. And the night passeth away, and the day cometh, and the sun also riseth. And all throughout this mansion, this mansion of life, the human imperfections of mankind reassert themselves. (*Exits. Lights up. Enter Tod, Tim, and a boy about 17.*)

BOY II. I have to go now.

TOD. Here's twenty. (*Hands him money.*)

BOY II. (*Touched.*) Thanks. Gee, thanks a lot. Usually it's ten, or even five. Would you like some green stamps?

TOD. We have so many. Thanks anyway.

BOY II. Gee, thanks. We at Grand Union are pleased to have served you. Call again.

TOD. We'll remember.

VIVIEN. (*Off-stage.*) Is that you, boys?

TIM. Yes, mother. (*Enter Vivien, on the arm of Martin.*)

TOD. Mother, I'd like you to meet Jack. He's a classmate from that school Tim and I went to for a week in Switzerland.

VIVIEN. Oh, how do you do, Jack. I've met several of your other classmates, I believe.

BOY II. Yes. Well, I must be going. Excuse me. (*Exits.*)

TOD. Goodbye.

VIVIEN. (*Wistfully.*) I thought I heard three of you in there last night.

MARTIN. Perhaps Madame would like her room moved.

VIVIEN. No, I like noises. As long as I know what they are. (*Scream off-stage.*) Like that. That's Margot discovering the dead body of her father. (*Enter Margot.*)

MARGOT. Miss Tyne has hanged herself!

VIVIEN. I was wrong. It was Miss Tyne. Well, why do you think she did it? Another depth of depression case, or did she get carried away putting on her tie?

TOD. Well, this comes as a surprise.

MARTIN. Mr. Jansen-Hubbell predicted her death to me last night before retiring.

MARGOT. And he did nothing to prevent it?

MARTIN. He's a dying man. What could he do?

VIVIEN. Is there any coffee, boys?

TIM. I think I'd like to sketch you sipping coffee. I'd call it Goddess Sipping Coffee While Awaiting the Death of Her Father.

VIVIEN. I like the goddess part.

TOD. It would make a good greeting card.

MARGOT. Is no one going to do anything about the dead woman?

MARTIN. I'll telephone the authorities.

MARGOT. (*Upset.*) Wait. Give me the key to the Tower. I want to see Grandma.

MARTIN. Miss Tyne keeps it around her neck. You can get it later. (*Exits.*)

MARGOT. I fear I could have helped her last night, and didn't. (*Enter Herbert.*) Father! Quick! Tell her!

VIVIEN. Why, Herbert, so you are here after all. Children, you know your father. Herbert, you've met the boys.

HERBERT. They've grown.

VIVIEN. Nonsense. You've just gotten smaller.

MARGOT. Tell her you hate her!

VIVIEN. Herbert, you're remarkably silent after all these years. Have you nothing to say?

HERBERT. How was Europe.

VIVIEN. Very pleasant. The boys had a nice puberty there. And such wonderful tans. Tod, show Herbert your tan. (*Tod lifts his shirt, showing his tanned stomach.*)

MARGOT. Father, please!

VIVIEN. Herbert, can you not still this voice of conscience that keeps echoing throughout the room?

HERBERT. (*Kneeling to her, fondly.*) Oh, Vivien, I hate you. (*He caresses her, his head on her breast, she holds him.*)

VIVIEN. Herbert, I'm touched. I had no idea I still had power over you. Look, children, your Father's come home to roost.

MARGOT. I hate you! I hate you all! (*She runs out.*)

VIVIEN. (*Tearing at the eyes.*) Oh, Herbert, we had good times, didn't we? Scurrying about the continent, knowing dukes and earls. Do you remember how you met me? You were just 17 and you went to your first brothel. I was just 14 and it was my first brothel too. My first night. And I remember the Madame, Madame Leore, said to me, she said, Vera—she got my name wrong even then—Vera, you'll turn many a trick in your day, but you'll never turn one like your first one. And so my heart was aglow and you came up to me and in your adolescent voice you said to me, "How much?" And I thought to myself that that was the most romantic thing I had ever heard. And so you and I retired to that little room with the cobwebs and the dank smell of urine and we sat on the bed. Is this your first? I asked, and when you said no I didn't believe you. And is this your first? you asked me, and when I said yes, you didn't believe me. And one of us was lying, and to this day I don't know which one it was, but I don't care because the night air was so fragrant and love was so new, and we were so young. So very, very young. And then you began very methodically to take off my clothes, which were soaked in perspiration from my busy day and from so many other bodies. And then I bit off your buttons, one by one, and your eyes grew larger at every pop. And then I took off your pants. I was very young, you understand, and I had never seen a man, not even a statue of one because they didn't have museums in those days and I wouldn't have gone even if they had. And so then your slender form got on top of my slender form and then—pump! Pump! PUMP! You pumped away, and I gave in to my first experience of love—Oh! Oh! Ohhhhhhh-Ohhhhhhhh. OHHHHHHHHHHHHHHHHHH. Uh.

Uh. And then when it was all over, I got off of you, and I looked into your blue eyes—your eyes were blue then—and I said in the pale, frightened voice of a school girl, "Herbert, it is you I love." (*Pause.*) Do you remember, Herbert? Herbert? (*Kindly.*) Children, I think your father's fallen asleep. (*She lets go of Herbert, and he falls to the ground.*) Oh. Has he had a stroke? Do you think it's a stroke? (*Enter Martin.*)

MARTIN. Your father is about to die, Madame. He wants to see you.

VIVIEN. Oh, dear! Do I look all right?

TOD. You look wonderful Mother!

TIM. Beautiful, dear.

VIVIEN. Oh. Thank you. Help me, Martin. (*Martin helps Vivien hobble off.*)

TOD. Why does Father only have one arm?

TIM. I don't know. War wound, I suppose. Tod?

TOD. (*Knowing what's coming.*) Yes.

TIM. About last night. I felt sort of funny. I mean, I'm used to having a third in with us and all, but last night I got the feeling you preferred the Grand Union to me.

TOD. Oh, for God's sake, are we going to go through this routine again? You're as bad as mother. You think you have to be worshipped all the time.

TIM. I don't want to be worshipped. I just want to know where we stand.

TOD. Oh, I hate this. Tim, you're my brother, and I like you better than anyone except myself, but that doesn't mean I don't want a little variety from time to time. For Christ's sake.

TIM. I think you're promiscuous.

TOD. Little hypocrite. Pot luck was your game anyway. You invented it.

TIM. Oh, go to hell.

TOD. Don't take it so hard. My wanting a little variety doesn't mean I prefer that grocery boy to my own brother. Now, for God's sake, let's shake hands and forget about it.

TIM. (*Grudgingly.*) All right. (*They shake hands. Enter Margaret with tea and graham crackers.*)

MARGARET. Oh, now, isn't that nice? Brothers, shaking hands. Here, I've brought some tea for my handsome boys. What's the matter with your father?

TOD. He's just tired.

TIM. It seems Grandad's about to kick off.

MARGARET. Is he now? Well, that'll be nice for him. No sense in senseless suffering, is there?

TOD. No. By definition.

MARGARET. That'll make two deaths today, what with that awful Miss Tyne bumping herself off. I never liked her, haven't for twelve years, won't start now that she's dead. I'm no hypocrite. Hope she rots in hell.

TIM. She seemed a mean sort.

MARGARET. Oh, she was. Not a kind word for anybody. Certainly not for me. And such a slanderous tongue she had, and a filthy mind to boot. Do you know what I heard her say to Martin after setting eyes on you two?

TOD. (*Taking tea, Tim likewise.*) No. What?

MARGARET. She said, those two is queer as the day they was born. And she said that being queer was one thing, and that incest was another, but to combine the two was a truly appalling perversion. And right she was, and a sick mind she had to even think of such a thing. God bless her guardian angel for seeing she hung herself. She's happier dead than alive brooding on such thoughts.

TIM. She had a sick imagination.

MARGARET. (*Coquette.*) And I said to myself, that even if you boys were acting funny together, it was only because the proper feminine companionship hadn't offered itself to you yet. I mean, after all, with your mother around all the time, I mean, a body is going to get pent up. We all have energies. And I thought, seeing how much I like both of you (*She starts to undo her blouse.*) I might be able to help you over this little hump in your lives. If you follow my meaning. (*Margaret's blouse is completely open now. She wears a bra.*) When you speak of this, and knowing you two like I do you probably will, be kind. Right?

TIM. Oh my God.

TOD. Ack. (*One or both of them throw their tea on her chest. She screams piercingly.*)

MARGARET. AAAAAHH! You bastards!

TIM. Go run 'em under the tap, love.

MARGARET. May Saint Peter piss on your grave! (*She exits screaming. Enter Margot.*)

MARGOT. What's the matter? Who's hurt?

TOD. Margaret sat on a tack.

MARGOT. What's the matter with father? (*Upset.*)

TIM. I'd forgotten. Mother thinks he might have had a stroke.

MARGOT. A stroke! Did anyone call a doctor?

TOD. A minute ago you told him you hated him. You're not very consistent.

MARGOT. Oh, please, he's all I've got. (*Enter Vivien, helped by Martin.*)

VIVIEN. Children, your grandfather has just died. He's left all his money to me, and he wishes all of us ill. He was a mean-spirited man all his life, and he remained so to the end.

MARGOT. Martin, call a doctor for my father.

VIVIEN. It is not necessary. Herbert's dead too. I felt his spirit leaving him right in the middle of my remembered youth.

MARGOT. (*Crying.*) He's all I have! He's all I have!

VIVIEN. He is all you *had*, Margot. Now you have nothing. You see, Margot, only the strong survive. I'm amazed that Herbert lasted as long as he did. I think your strength kept him alive for a while; for although I don't like you, you do have some strength. But I guess it wasn't enough, and now he's dead.

MARGOT. What am I to do?

VIVIEN. Leave my sight forever. Attach yourself elsewhere. And remember, I placed you in an orphanage once. Don't tempt me to do it again. (*She sits.*) Come, Tim, sketch your mother in mourning. Tod, write a poem about your mother in grief. (*Martin removes Herbert's body.*)

MARGOT. (*Following body.*) I hate you, father! You're weak! Grandma! Grandma! (*She exits.*)

VIVIEN. It will have been an emotionally exhausting day, I fear. (*Vivien, Tod, and Tim remain on stage, quietly posing, sketching, writing. D. C. is spotlight, becomes the Tower. Cry of "Grandma!" off-stage. Enter Mrs. Jansen-Hubbell, her hands still tied, several bruises on her head. Enter Margot, frenzied.*)

MARGOT. Grandma! Grandma. They're both dead! And I hate them both. Oh, please, be lucid. I know you're just pretending to be crazy. (*She begins to untie Mrs. J.-H's hands.*) Grandma, say something. What shall I do? I don't feel strong anymore. Say something. Do you remember when I was a little girl? You made me cookies the day you went crazy, and you said, "Margot, whenever things get you down, just have a nice glass of milk and a couple of cookies." And then right after that you went crazy, do you remember? Grandma, say something. Please say something! (*Pause.*)

MRS. J-H. (*Shrieking.*) DON'T DEPEND ON PEOPLE! (*She reaches out to Margot and strangles her to death. Then exits, wailing. Lights off "Tower"; Margot's dead body remains til end of play.*)

TIM. Don't move, mother. I can't sketch you.

TOD. I think you should get rid of Margaret.

VIVIEN. Whatever you think best, dear. You know, as your grandfather died, he called me evil. And he said he was evil. But I don't think people are evil really. I think we're all misguided. I mean, everybody wants love. That was Miss Tyne's problem. She wanted money. If she'd wanted love instead, think how happy she would have been. Everyone has the right to expect love. Everyone wants love. What's that famous poem? "It's love, it's love, it's love, it's love." Of course, everyone can't have love. Take Margot. I was never meant to love her. She's a well meaning thing, but I had my boys and my own life, and she was conceived by mistake, as a means to facilitate sleep. Your father lost his boyish charm as time went on. Oh, well, it's been a hard day, but we can relax tonight, and tomorrow we'll return to the continent. This house has too many memories.

TOD. (*Looking at Tim.*) Do you want anything from the supermarket?

VIVIEN. (*Afraid.*) I'm sure there's plenty in the kitchen.

TOD. (*To Tim.*) Do you?

TIM. (*Angry.*) What's the matter with leftovers?

TOD. Leftovers are nice and cozy and a comfort, but fresh food adds spice to any table.

VIVIEN. (*Sadly.*) Children, mother hates metaphor.

TIM. (*To Tod.*) Very well. But not Grand Union. Is that understood?

TOD. Suits me. We haven't tried the Stop 'n' Shop.

VIVIEN. Maybe East Haddam doesn't have a Stop 'n' Shop.

TIM. All right. We can phone from upstairs. (*They start to exit.*)

VIVIEN. I'm sure there's plenty of food in the kitchen.

TOD. (*Smiling.*) The food in the kitchen is burned.

TIM. See you later, mother. (*They exit.*)

VIVIEN. Goodnight, my twins. Rejoice in being two. For loneliness is a terrible thing. (*To herself.*) My children are so artistic. Wonderful children of a wonderful mother. (*To herself.*) I can't help feeling sorry, though, that they're not really a bit nicer. Of course, I'm not all that nice either, I suppose, by some people's standards. But I don't think one should criticize. Let he who is without sin cast the first stone, Christ said. So they tell me. Ah, Tod, Tim. So lucky to be two. I even rather wish Herbert were alive tonight. Oh well. One does the best one can. That's what I always say. And if you're lonely one moment, you forget it the next, so it couldn't be too bad, because you forget it. Yes. I think that's the way it is. (*Sings softly to herself as lights dim.*)

PROPERTY LIST

Telephone, on stand
Butterscotch pudding
Dead rat
Gong (hand held, or on set)
Sketch pad and pencil (Tim)
Tea service, tray
Graham crackers
Grocery packages
Grocery charge pad and pencil
Microphone, tape recorder
Book
Frying pan
Scouring pad
Money (20 dollar bill) ⎱
Writing pad and pen ⎰ (Tod)

'DENTITY CRISIS

'DENTITY CRISIS was presented by the Yale Repertory Theatre, New Haven, Connecticut, on a double bill with "Guess Work" by Robert Auletta, on October 13, 1978. The direction of " 'dentity Crisis" was by Frank Torok, scenery by Michael H. Yeargan, costumes by Marjorie Graf, lighting by Robert Jared. The cast was as follows:

JANE .... Katherine Clarke
EDITH .... Darcy Pulliam
ROBERT .... Mark Linn-Baker
MR. SUMMERS .... David K. Miller
WOMAN .... Nancy Mayans

SETTING

The setting of this play could be any living room with a couch, table, chair, etc. Because the living room has been presumably chosen and decorated by Edith, who is fairly insane, there should be some odd things about the decor.

The production at the Yale Repertory Theatre chose (partly due to its wide stage) to have a bizarrely symmetrical set: identical couches, chair and table Stage Left, and Stage Right; there was a piano and piano bench Upstage Center. There were doors, identical, Left and Right.

On the wall there were five large, framed photographs: four utterly identical ones of Robert, two on either side; and one of Jane, in the Center above the piano.

Due to the extreme number of personalities that "Robert" turns out to possess, the four photos of him strike me as an excellent idea.

The symmetrical, mirror-like image of the two couches, two chairs, etc. strikes me as successfully odd and worked well in the Yale Rep production. It doesn't have the thematic resonance of the four photos of Robert, however; and so if your stage was not all that wide, or if you wanted to experiment with either a more realistic living room, or with a differently odd one (one that mixed styles of furniture radically, for instance), you should feel free to experiment.

One prop note you might find helpful: the "tables" in the Yale Rep production were actually square cubes that opened on top, and inside were kept all of Edith and Robert's paraphernalia. This was both useful for staging purposes, and made sense thematically as well (Edith and Robert keeping all their "toys" in a sort of toy chest).

> SCENE: *Living room. Jane, the daughter, in disheveled bathrobe, lies on the couch. She is extremely depressed and sits paging steadily through a* Time Magazine, *not looking at it at all.*

VOICE. (*Offstage.*) Cuckoo. Cuckoo. (*Enter Edith, carrying a bag of groceries and a dress in a dry cleaner's bag. Dress is very badly stained with blood.*)
EDITH. Hello, dear, I'm back. Did you miss me? Say yes.

(*Pause.*) Of course you missed me. A daughter always misses her mother. You're less depressed today, aren't you? I can tell. (*Puts bag down.*) I got your dress back. I'm afraid the stains didn't come out. You should have heard the lady at the cleaners. What did she do, slash her thighs with a razor blade? she said. I had to admit you had. Really, dear, I've never heard of anyone doing that. It was so awful when your father and I went into the bathroom together to brush our teeth and saw you perched up on the toilet, your pretty white dress over your head, slashing away at your thighs. I don't think your father had ever seen your thighs before, and I hope he never will again, at least not under those unpleasant conditions. I mean, what could have possessed you? No one in our family has ever attempted suicide before now, and no one since either. It's a sign of defeat, and no one should do it. You know what I think? Jane? Jane?

JANE. What?

EDITH. I don't think you ever attempted suicide at all. That's what I think.

JANE. How do you explain the stains then?

EDITH. I don't. (*Laughs merrily.*) I always say stains will explain themselves, and if they don't then there's nothing can be done about it. (*Edith empties the grocery bag on the table. It is filled with loose potato chips, which Edith playfully arranges as if it is some sort of food sculpture.*)

JANE. I did attempt suicide.

EDITH. No, dear, you didn't. A daughter doesn't contradict her mother.

VOICE. Cuckoo, cuckoo.

JANE. Did you hear the voice of my therapist just then?

EDITH. No, dear. (*Listens.*) Ah, now I hear it. He's saying what a fine daughter I have. (*Enter Robert.*)

ROBERT. Mother! I'm home.

EDITH. Oh, Jane, it's your brother. (*Edith and Robert kiss passionately and long. Jane is very upset and rips up the plastic covering on her dress.*)

ROBERT. Darling, darling.

EDITH. Oh, Dwayne, this is mad. We're got to stop meeting like this. Your father will find out.

JANE. I'll tell him!

EDITH. Jane, you'd never do anything like that.

ROBERT. I'm mad for you. I find you . . . exciting. (*They kiss.*)
EDITH. (*Looking off.*) Quick, there's the postman. Act busy.
(*Robert and Edith smash the potato chips on the table with their fists. Then they brush the crushed chips into a waste basket with a little broom.*)
EDITH. There, he's gone.
ROBERT. (*Holding her.*) Oh, why must you taunt me? Let's get married.
EDITH. We have different blood types.
ROBERT. Oh, mother, I love you. (*They embrace.*)
EDITH. Oh, my God. Here comes your father. (*Robert, with no change of costume and without exiting or re-entering—becomes the father.*)
ROBERT. Edith, what are you doing?
EDITH. Oh, Arthur, I was just finishing off my morning shopping.
ROBERT. And how is our daughter?
JANE. You're not my father.
EDITH. Don't contradict your father. You love your father, Jane.
JANE. He's my brother.
EDITH. Dwayne is your brother, dear.
ROBERT. Has she been seeing that psychologist of hers?
EDITH. Well, not socially.
ROBERT. Good. (*Shouting at Jane.*) I don't ever want to hear of you dating a psychologist again.
JANE. I never have!
EDITH. Of course not, dear. You obey your father. You're a good daughter.
ROBERT. Not like some I could mention.
EDITH. No.
ROBERT. I could mention some.
EDITH. You could.
ROBERT. I could. I will.
EDITH. Now?
ROBERT. Now. Frances, Lucia, Henrietta, Charmant, Dolores, Loretta, and Peggy.
EDITH. Listen to your father, Jane.
ROBERT. No more of this slashing your thighs, young lady. I don't think that psychologist would ever go out with you again if he knew you were slashing your thighs.
JANE. I don't go out with my psychologist.

71

EDITH. Of course you don't. He has a wife and sixteen children. You're a good girl. You listen to your father.

JANE. (*To Robert.*) You're not my father.

EDITH. Jane, you know he's your father.

JANE. If you're my father, you must be close to fifty.

ROBERT. I am close to fifty.

JANE. Let me see your driver's license.

ROBERT. Here. (*Hands it to her.*)

JANE. (*Reads it.*) This says you're fifty. How did you get them to put that down?

EDITH. The truth is the truth no matter how you look at it, Jane.

JANE. How come you don't look fifty?

EDITH. Your father never looked his age. Most girls would be pleased that their fathers looked young.

ROBERT. Most girls are pleased.

EDITH. Jane's pleased you look young, aren't you, Jane? Don't you think Arthur looks young for his age, Grandad?

ROBERT. Eh? What?

EDITH. (*Shouting.*) Don't you think Arthur looks young, Grandad!

ROBERT. (*Smiling senilely.*) Yes, yes. Breakfast.

EDITH. Poor Grandad can't hear a thing.

JANE. Where's father?

EDITH. Isn't he here? That's funny. I didn't hear the door close.

JANE. Grandad, mother is having an affair with Dwayne!

ROBERT. (*Not hearing.*) What?

EDITH. He can't hear you. Besides you mustn't make up stories. I don't. Oh, listen to the doorbell. (*Bell rings. Enter Mr. Summers, the psychologist and the previous offstage voice.*) Why, Jane, it's your psychologist. (*To Summers.*) I recognized you from your photos. Jane has plastered her walls with your pictures. I don't know why.

SUMMERS. How do you do? You must be Jane's mother.

EDITH. Yes. I'm Edith Fromage. You probably saw my photo in the papers when you were a little boy. I invented cheese in France in the early portion of the century.

SUMMERS. In what way did you invent cheese?

EDITH. In every way. And this is my son, Dwayne Fromage.

ROBERT. How do you do, sir?

72

SUMMERS. How do you do? I didn't realize Jane's last name was Fromage.

EDITH. It isn't. I had Jane by another husband. A Mr. Carrot.

JANE. My name isn't Carrot.

EDITH. That's right, dear. It's *Jane* Carrot. (*Whispers.*) Jane's very overwrought today. The stains wouldn't come out of her dress.

SUMMERS. Oh, I'm sorry.

EDITH. You think you're sorry. You should have seen the woman at the cleaners. I thought we'd have to chain her to the floor.

ROBERT. Perhaps Mr. Summers is hungry.

EDITH. Oh, forgive me. (*Offers him waste basket of crushed chips.*)

SUMMERS. No thank you.

EDITH. Then how about some entertainment? Jane, play the piano for Mr. Summers.

JANE. I don't play the piano.

EDITH. Of course you do. I've heard you many times. You play very well.

JANE. I've never played the piano.

EDITH. Jane, Mr. Summers would enjoy your playing. Please play.

JANE. I don't know how!

EDITH. (*Angry.*) How do you know? Have you ever tried?

JANE. No.

EDITH. There. You see then. (*To Summers.*) Cello is her real instrument, but we never talk about it.

ROBERT. Please play, Jane. (*Jane walks hesitatingly to the piano, sits. Pause. Makes some noise on keyboard, obviously can't play, starts to cry.*)

JANE. I don't know how to play piano!

EDITH. But you do! Why else would we have one? No one else in the house plays.

JANE. I don't remember taking lessons.

EDITH. You probably forgot due to all this strain. (*To Summers.*) You talk to her. She seems in a state. (*To Robert.*) Come on, dear. Call me if you want me, Mr. Summers. (*Robert and Edith kiss, then exit.*)

JANE. (*At piano.*) I don't *remember* taking piano lessons.

SUMMERS. Maybe you've repressed it. (*Sits.*) My wife gave me the message about your attempting suicide. Why did you do it, Jane?

JANE. I can't stand it. My mother says she's invented cheese and I start to think maybe she has. There's a man living in the house and I'm not sure whether he's my brother or my father or my grandfather. I can't be sure of anything anymore.

SUMMERS. You're talking quite rationally now. And your self-doubts are a sign of health. The truly crazy person never thinks he's crazy. Now explain to me what led up to your attempted suicide.

JANE. Well, a few days ago I woke up and I heard this voice saying, "It wasn't enough."

SUMMERS. Did you recognize the voice?

JANE. Not at first. But then it started to come back to me. When I was eight years old, someone brought me to a theatre with lots of other children. We had come to see a production of "Peter Pan." And I remember something seemed wrong with the whole production, odd things kept happening. Like when the children would fly, the ropes would keep breaking and the actors would come thumping to the ground and they'd have to be carried off by the stage hands. There seemed to be an unlimited supply of understudies to take the children's places, and then *they'd* fall to the ground. And then the crocodile that chases Captain Hook seemed to be a real crocodile, it wasn't an actor, and at one point it fell off the stage, crushing several children in the front row.

SUMMERS. What happened to the children?

JANE. Several understudies came and took their places in the audience. And from scene to scene Wendy seemed to get fatter and fatter until finally by the second act she was immobile and had to be moved with a cart.

SUMMERS. Where does the voice fit in?

JANE. The voice belonged to the actress playing Peter Pan. You remember how in the second act Tinkerbell drinks some poison that Peter's about to drink, in order to save him? And then Peter turns to the audience and he says that Tinkerbell's going to die because not enough people believe in fairies, but that if everybody in the audience claps real hard to show that they *do* believe in fairies, then maybe Tinkerbell won't die. And so then all the children started to clap. We clapped very hard and very long. My palms hurt and even started to bleed I clapped so hard. Then suddenly the actress playing Peter Pan turned to the audience and she said, "That wasn't enough. You didn't clap hard enough. Tinkerbell's dead." Uh . . . well, and . . . and then everyone started to cry. The actress stalked offstage and refused to continue with the play, and they finally had to bring down the curtain. No one could see anything through all the tears, and the ushers had to come help the children up the aisles and out into the street. I don't think any of us were ever the same after that experience.

SUMMERS. How do you think this affected you?

JANE. Well it certainly turned me against theatre; but more damagingly, I think it's warped my sense of life. You know—nothing seems worth trying if Tinkerbell's just going to die.

SUMMERS. And so you wanted to die like Tinkerbell.

JANE. Yes.

SUMMERS. (*With importance.*) Jane. I have to bring my wife to the hospital briefly this afternoon, so I have to go now. But I want you to hold on, and I'll check back later today. I think you're going to be all right, but I think you need a complete rest; so when I come back we'll talk about putting you somewhere for a while.

JANE. You mean committing me.

SUMMERS. No. This would just be a rest home, a completely temporary thing. Tinkerbell just needs her batteries recharged, that's all. Now you just make your mind a blank, and I'll be back as soon as I can.

JANE. Thank you. I'll try to stay quiet 'til you return. (*Enter Edith.*)

EDITH. Oh, you're leaving. Won't you have some of my cheese first?

SUMMERS. Thank you, Mrs. Fromage, but I have to go now. Please see to it that your daughter stays quiet.

EDITH. Oh, you can rely on me.

SUMMERS. (*To Jane.*) Chin up. (*Exits.*)

EDITH. Jane, dear, I've brought you some sheet music. I thought maybe if you got settled on where middle C was, it might all come back to you.

JANE. Please leave me alone.

EDITH. I don't know why you've turned against the piano.

JANE. (*Suddenly sharp.*) Well you know my one love was always the cello.

EDITH. (*Realizing Jane is being devious.*) A good daughter does not speak to her mother in that tone. I'm sure you didn't mean that. When you are ready to play the piano, let me know. Oh, there's the doorbell. (*Bell rings. Enter Robert.*)

ROBERT. (*French accent.*) Ah, Madame Fromage.

EDITH. Oh, Count. How nice. I don't think you've met my daughter. Jane, dear, this is the Count de Rochelay, my new benefactor.

ROBERT. How do you do, Mademoiselle? My people and I are most anxious for your mother to make a comeback. All the time, the people of France say, whatever happened to Edith Fromage who gave us cheese? It is time she left her solitude and returned to the spotlight and invented something new. And so I come to your charming Mama and I convince her to answer the call of the people of France.

EDITH. Jane, say hello to the count.

JANE. Hello.

EDITH. (*Whispers.*) You have to forgive her. She's sulking because she's forgotten how to play the piano. (*He embraces her.*)

ROBERT. Madame Fromage, I love you!

EDITH. Please! I don't want my son or husband to hear you!

ROBERT. (*Whispers.*) Madame Fromage, I love you. (*Kisses her.*)

EDITH. Not now. First I must invent something new. Have you the ingredients? (*Robert has paper bag. Edith takes out a family size loaf of* Wonder Bread *and makes a stack of 6 slices. Then she takes a banana from the bag and rams it into the center of the stack of bread.*)

ROBERT. Bravo, Madame!

EDITH. Voila! I have invented banana bread.

ROBERT. Bravo! Let us make love to celebrate!

EDITH. Please, my son or husband might hear.

ROBERT. (*Deaf.*) Eh?

EDITH. Shush, Grandad. Go down to the cellar.

ROBERT. Madame Fromage, France will thank you for this.

EDITH. And I will thank France. It is moments like these when I feel most alive. (*Robert carries Edith off.*)

ROBERT. Vive Madame Fromage! (*Jane at piano hits middle C several times. Lights dim, slowly to blackout. As they do, the light of a flashlight flashes about the stage as Tinkerbell.*)

EDITH'S VOICE. (*Offstage, as Peter Pan.*) Tink, are you all right, Tink? Tinkerbell? (*Light of Tinkerbell starts to blink on and off.*)

JANE. Don't die! (*Jane's solitary clapping is heard in darkness. Tinkerbell's light goes off.*)

EDITH'S VOICE. (*Off, in darkness.*) That wasn't enough. She's dead. Tinkerbell's dead.

BLACKOUT

SCENE: *Lights up on Jane seated at piano with a paper bag over her head.*

VOICE. (*Offstage; Summers.*) Cuckoo, cuckoo. (*Enter Robert.*)

ROBERT. Have you seen your mother?

JANE. (*Under bag.*) To whom am I speaking?

ROBERT. Take off the bag and see. (*She takes off the bag.*)

JANE. To whom am I speaking?

ROBERT. Don't act odd, Jane. Tell your father you'll be normal.

JANE. I'll be normal.

ROBERT. I'll be normal, comma, Father.

JANE. I'll be normal, comma, Father. (*Enter Edith.*)

EDITH. Oh, there you are, children.

ROBERT. Mother, don't leave me for that Count. Edith, what is Dwayne talking about?

EDITH. I'm sure I don't know, Arthur. (*Whispers to Robert.*) Don't let your father hear about the Count.

ROBERT. Mother, I love you. Edith, what did you just whisper to Dwayne?

EDITH. Oh, nothing, dear. Just that Grandad's hearing is getting worse. Look, I've invented banana bread, aren't you proud of me?

ROBERT. Congratulations, Edith. Gee, Mom. (*Deaf.*) What?

EDITH. (*Shouting.*) Banana bread, Grandad!

ROBERT. It's too early for bed.

JANE. I only see two people.

EDITH. I'm sure you see more than that, dear. Oh, the doorbell. (*Doorbell. Enter a Woman.*)

WOMAN. Hello, Mrs. Fromage. How's Jane?

EDITH. Much better. Jane, a visitor.

JANE. Who are you?

WOMAN. I'm your psychologist, Mr. Summers.

JANE. I don't . . . understand.

WOMAN. I guess it's confusing, but I didn't want to tell you earlier. I got a sex change this afternoon.

JANE. I don't believe you.

WOMAN. It's quite true. My wife can substantiate. (*Calls.*) Harriet. (*Enter Mr. Summers.*)

SUMMERS. Yes, dear.

WOMAN. Explain to Jane that I am Mr. Summers.

SUMMERS. How do you do, Jane? My husband has told me so much about you and your neuroses. You're one of my favorite cases.

JANE. I don't understand.

WOMAN. It simply seemed that the magic had gone out of our marriage, and that we both needed a change.

JANE. You should have told me. You should have prepared me.

WOMAN. I didn't want to spring it on you too quickly.

EDITH. I think it's very courageous of you both.

SUMMERS. Thank you.

WOMAN. (*To Summers.*) Harriet, is that a banana in your trousers, or are you just happy to see me?

SUMMERS. It's a banana. (*Takes a banana out of his trousers, to Jane.*) They haven't fitted me with any male appendages yet, so I've been trying everything to get the hang of it. I think a banana's too large.

EDITH. Might I have the banana?

SUMMERS. Surely. (*Edith makes another thing of banana bread, quickly.*)

WOMAN. I've been wondering how my patients would react to the change.

ROBERT. Mother, I love you.

EDITH. Hush, dear, they'll hear you.

WOMAN. (*To Jane.*) Now tell me about the dream about the Peter Pan play again.

JANE. It wasn't a dream. It was a memory from my childhood.

WOMAN. Oh, I thought you told me it was a dream.

JANE. No, I didn't.

EDITH. I was listening at the door and feel sure you said it was a dream. Didn't you, dear?

JANE. It wasn't a dream, and I didn't say it was. (*To Woman.*) And I didn't tell you about it anyway. (*Pointing to Summers.*) I told him.

WOMAN. But you've never met Harriet until this very minute.

JANE. You're pulling a trick on me. (*Summers whispers to Woman.*)

WOMAN. Oh, my God. Mrs. Fromage, have you any glue?

EDITH. Yes. I invented some this morning.

ROBERT. Ah, Madame Fromage, bravo for you.

EDITH. (*Handing Woman bottle.*) I call it mucilage.

WOMAN. (*Squeezing some on her breast.*) You must excuse me. My wife just noticed that one of my breasts was slipping off.

EDITH. Could I get you a melon?

WOMAN. No thank you. This should do it. Modern surgery is a wonder these days, but it can be sloppily done sometimes.

JANE. I don't think you can help me.

WOMAN. Oh dear. You see, Harriet.

SUMMERS. I see.

WOMAN. A hostile reaction to my change. Jane, dear, I'm just as capable as I was before.

JANE. I think you're crazy.

ROBERT. What? Eh?

JANE. Shut up! You're not my father.

EDITH. Of course not. He's your grandfather.

JANE. Let me see his drivers' license.

EDITH. He doesn't drive. It wouldn't be wise.

SUMMERS. Oh my God! (*Scratches all over.*)

WOMAN. Harriet, what's the matter?

SUMMERS. I feel so unused to these clothes. The pants rub my legs and the shoes are too heavy and I miss my breasts.

WOMAN. Harriet. Please. We can talk about this after my session with Jane.

SUMMERS. Walter, we can't. I feel very nervous all of a sudden. May I see you in the other room for a second?

WOMAN. Very well. Mrs. Fromage, might my wife and I talk in your bedroom for a second?

EDITH. Surely. Don't step on the potato chips.

WOMAN. I'll be right back, Jane.

SUMMERS. Do excuse me. I guess I'm making the transition poorly. (*Woman and Summers exit.*)

ROBERT. Madame Fromage, now that your husband and son and father have gone down to the cellar for a minute, let me ask you to become my wife. We could live in France, your true home, where the people love you for the great gift you have given them. (*Jane puts her hands over her ears.*)

EDITH. What about my husband and the rest of my family?

ROBERT. Bring them all along. I have a big heart.

EDITH. That's most generous, but I must consult my daughter. Jane, did you hear the Count's offer. (*She takes Jane's hands off her ears.*)

JANE. No.

EDITH. Yes you did. Do you approve?

JANE. No.

EDITH. Yes you do. Do you want to come with us to France?

JANE. No.

EDITH. Yes you do. Oh, Count, Jane's agreed to everything.

ROBERT. Darling!

EDITH. My count! (*They embrace.*)

ROBERT. (*Suddenly.*) Mother, what is the meaning of this? Edith!

EDITH. Now, Dwayne, Arthur.

ROBERT. Edith, I'm shocked. (*Count.*) Don't jump to any hasty presumptions, Monsieur Fromage.

EDITH. Arthur, the Count and I were discussing my going back to the stage.

ROBERT. You're used that story before.

EDITH. Never.

ROBERT. Yes you have.

EDITH. Albert, you're belligerent.

ROBERT. Arthur.

EDITH. Arthur, you're belligerent.

ROBERT. Father, don't use that tone with my mother.

EDITH. Dwayne, don't speak crossly to your father.

ROBERT. (*Count.*) I think it is terrible any of you speak rudely to Madame Fromage. (*He coughs violently.*)

EDITH. Oh, dear, Grandad's having a coughing fit. Dwayne, run and get your grandfather some water.

ROBERT. (*Stops coughing.*) You're just trying to distract from the issue. (*Coughs.*)

EDITH. Your grandfather's choking. How can you be so cruel?

ROBERT. (*Stern.*) Listen to your mother. (*Coughs.*) Mother, we've got to get this settled first. Who do you love more—me, father, or the Count?

EDITH. Do you mean more frequently, or in greater degree?

ROBERT. Degree. (*Coughs, drops to the floor.*)

EDITH. Oh my God, he's fainted.

ROBERT. Good God, Edith, is he dead? (*Count, stooping down.*) No. He is just sleeping.

EDITH. Oh good.

ROBERT. Well, who do you love?

EDITH. Dwayne, when you ask a woman that you ask her to explain her existence. And so I will. Dwayne, I love you as a mother loves a son, as a wife loves a husband, and as a woman loves a lover. Arthur, I love you as a wife loves a son, a husband loves a lover, and a mother loves a woman. Count, I love you as a son loves a husband, as a lover loves a mother, as a wife loves a brother. It's one for all, and all for one. There, are you satisfied?

ROBERT. Mother, you're wonderful. (*Kisses her.*) Edith, I'm touched. (*Kisses her.*) Madame, you are charmant. (*Kisses her. Enter Woman and Summers. They have switched clothes: Woman wears Summers' clothes, he wears hers. That is, Summers is dressed like a woman; the Woman is dressed like a man.*)

JANE. Oh God, help me.

WOMAN. Now Jane, there's no need to overreact. Harriet just felt uncomfortable.

SUMMERS. (*Looking at his flat chest.*) I don't look like I used to. Not at all. (*Places a stray banana in his bosom.*)

EDITH. I don't think I've introduced you properly. This is my husband Arthur.

ROBERT. How do you do?

WOMAN. How do you do? I'm Mr. Summers and this is my husband Harriet.

SUMMERS. How do you do?

ROBERT. I do very well, thank you.

EDITH. And this is my son Dwayne.

SUMMERS. How do you do? I'm Mr. Summers and this is my wife Walter.

ROBERT. How do you do?

EDITH. And this is the Count de Rochelay.

ROBERT. Comment ca va?

81

WOMAN. Tres bien, merci. Je m'appele Jacqueline, et voici mon fromage, Claud.

SUMMERS. Bonjour, bonjour.

EDITH. And this is my new invention, banana bread. I dedicate it to Jane, my wonderful daughter. I call the recipe Banana Bread Jane.

ROBERT. Did you hear that, Jane?

JANE. I don't know who you are.

EDITH. Come. Let us taste of the banana bread. Jane, it's your birthday, you cut the first piece.

JANE. It isn't my birthday.

EDITH. It is. We've been wishing you happy birthday all day.

ROBERT. Happy birthday, Jane. We're going to get the piano tuned for you.

JANE. Who are you?

ROBERT. What? Eh?

SUMMERS. Joyeux Noel, Jane.

WOMAN. Allez-vous a la bibliotheque?

EDITH. Jane, cut the banana bread. (*The Woman and Summers sing the Marseillaise. Jane takes a knife and goes to cut the bread.*) That's right, dear. (*Jane suddenly takes the knife and whacks off the top of the banana sticking out of the bread.*)

WOMAN. (*Screams in agony, holds between her legs.*) That's a very inconsiderate thing for you to do. I'm going to have nightmares now.

SUMMERS. Jane, you've upset my wife.

JANE. I thought she was your husband!

EDITH. Jane, I'd like you to meet my daughter Jane.

SUMMERS. How do you do, Jane?

ROBERT. How do you do?

WOMAN. How do you do?

JANE. I don't understand. Which one is Jane?

EDITH. Don't play games with me. You know which one.

JANE. No I don't! (*Edith, Robert, Woman, and Summers keep shaking hands, introducing themselves to each other over and over. However, now instead of saying their names, they each are singing different French songs to one another. Robert and Summers sing "Freres Jacques"; Woman sings "The Marseillaise", Edith sings "Sur le pont d'Avignon" or some other song in French. The whole thing, rather cheerful sounding, sounds like a music box gone*)

mad. Jane runs to the side and screams.) Help! HELP! HELP!
(*Lights go out. The French singing continues in the blackout. The singing fades after a bit, and the lights come up again, with only Jane and Edith on stage. Jane is on the couch. Her hands are tied together, or else she's in a strait jacket; and tape is across her mouth. Edith sits watching her.*)

VOICES. (*That of Summers and Woman alternatively.*) Cuckoo, cuckoo. Cuckoo, cuckoo.

EDITH. Oh, time for the bandage to come off. (*Takes tape off Jane's mouth.*) How are you, Jane? (*Jane smiles.*) Jane? How are you?

JANE. Jane isn't here.

EDITH. Oh. Then who are you?

JANE. I'm Jane's mother.

EDITH. How do you do? I'm Edith Fromage. I invented cheese and banana bread.

JANE. I'm Emily Carrot. I discovered radium in carrots.

EDITH. Really? That's the last time I ever put them in a salad.

JANE. Untie me.

EDITH. Certainly, Emily. (*Does so.*) I was about to make something good to eat for my husband, son, father, and lover. They're tired of cheese and banana bread. Would you help me cook something?

JANE. Yes, Edith.

EDITH. What should we make?

JANE. Let's make a child.

EDITH. I don't know if I have a big enough bowl.

JANE. That's all right. We don't have to put the yeast in. We'll make a small child.

EDITH. Oh fine. What ingredients do we need?

JANE. Cheese and banana bread.

EDITH. I have that. (*They begin to put ingredients into a vat.*)

JANE. Lots of eggs.

EDITH. Lots of eggs.

JANE. Olives for the eyes.

EDITH. Olives.

JANE. Wheat germ for the hair.

EDITH. Oh really? I didn't know that.

JANE. Oh yes. When I was in Germany, we made the most beautiful children with wheat germ hair.

EDITH. Emily, dear?

JANE. Yes?

EDITH. Welcome home. (*They embrace. Enter Woman and Summers holding hands.*)

WOMAN and SUMMERS. (*Jn unison.*) At this point it seems in order to offer the psychological key to this evening's performance.

SUMMERS. Jane's repressed fear of carrots, indicated by her refusal to acknowledge her proper surname, mirrored a disorder in her libidinous regions . . .

WOMAN. . . . which in turn made her unable to distinguish between her father and her brother and her grandfather; as long as she could not recognize to whom she was speaking . . .

SUMMERS. . . . she would not have to react to them sexually. When Jane finally released the forces of her libido by whacking off the banana bread . . .

WOMAN. . . . she freed her imprisoned personality . . .

SUMMERS. . . . and enabled herself to face . . .

WOMAN. . . . her festering . . .

SUMMERS. . . . competition . . .

WOMAN. . . . with her mother. (*Woman and Summers kiss.*)

SUMMERS. The moral of the play is that through the miracle of modern psychology . . .

WOMAN. . . . man is able . . .

SUMMERS. . . . to solve his problems . . .

WOMAN. . . . and be happy.

BOTH. Thank you and good night. (*They kiss and keep kissing. Jane and Edith continue baking. Enter Robert.*)

ROBERT. Identity. I dentity, you dentity, he she or it dentities. We dentity, you dentity, they dentity. Cuckoo. Cuckoo. Cuckoo. (*As the Count.*) I dentity. (*As Dwayne.*) you dentity, (*As grandfather.*) he she or it dentities . . .

LIGHTS FADE

PROPERTY LIST

Couch
Bag of groceries (potato chips)
Blood-stained dress, in dry-cleaner's bag
Waste basket
Whisk broom
Piano
Bag of groceries (loaf of bread and bananas)
Paper bag
Bottle of glue
Strait jacket
Large kitchen knife

NEW PLAYS

★ **SHEL'S SHORTS by Shel Silverstein.** Lauded poet, songwriter and author of children's books, the incomparable Shel Silverstein's short plays are deeply infused with the same wicked sense of humor that made him famous. "...[a] childlike honesty and twisted sense of humor." *–Boston Herald.* "...terse dialogue and an absurdity laced with a tang of dread give [*Shel's Shorts*] more than a trace of Samuel Beckett's comic existentialism." *–Boston Phoenix.* [flexible casting] ISBN: 0-8222-1897-6

★ **AN ADULT EVENING OF SHEL SILVERSTEIN by Shel Silverstein.** Welcome to the darkly comic world of Shel Silverstein, a world where nothing is as it seems and where the most innocent conversation can turn menacing in an instant. These ten imaginative plays vary widely in content, but the style is unmistakable. "...[*An Adult Evening*] shows off Silverstein's virtuosic gift for wordplay...[and] sends the audience out...with a clear appreciation of human nature as perverse and laughable." *–NY Times.* [flexible casting] ISBN: 0-8222-1873-9

★ **WHERE'S MY MONEY? by John Patrick Shanley.** A caustic and sardonic vivisection of the institution of marriage, laced with the author's inimitable razor-sharp wit. "...Shanley's gift for acid-laced one-liners and emotionally tumescent exchanges is certainly potent..." *–Variety.* "...lively, smart, occasionally scary and rich in reverse wisdom." *–NY Times.* [3M, 3W] ISBN: 0-8222-1865-8

★ **A FEW STOUT INDIVIDUALS by John Guare.** A wonderfully screwy comedy-drama that figures Ulysses S. Grant in the throes of writing his memoirs, surrounded by a cast of fantastical characters, including the Emperor and Empress of Japan, the opera star Adelina Patti and Mark Twain. "Guare's smarts, passion and creativity skyrocket to awesome heights..." *–Star Ledger.* "...precisely the kind of good new play that you might call an everyday miracle...every minute of it is fresh and newly alive..." *–Village Voice.* [10M, 3W] ISBN: 0-8222-1907-7

★ **BREATH, BOOM by Kia Corthron.** A look at fourteen years in the life of Prix, a Bronx native, from her ruthless girl-gang leadership at sixteen through her coming to maturity at thirty. "...vivid world, believable and eye-opening, a place worthy of a dramatic visit, where no one would want to live but many have to." *–NY Times.* "...rich with humor, terse vernacular strength and gritty detail..." *–Variety.* [1M, 9W] ISBN: 0-8222-1849-6

★ **THE LATE HENRY MOSS by Sam Shepard.** Two antagonistic brothers, Ray and Earl, are brought together after their father, Henry Moss, is found dead in his seedy New Mexico home in this classic Shepard tale. "...His singular gift has been for building mysteries out of the ordinary ingredients of American family life..." *–NY Times.* "...rich moments ...Shepard finds gold." *–LA Times.* [7M, 1W] ISBN: 0-8222-1858-5

★ **THE CARPETBAGGER'S CHILDREN by Horton Foote.** One family's history spanning from the Civil War to WWII is recounted by three sisters in evocative, intertwining monologues. "...bittersweet music—[a] rhapsody of ambivalence...in its modest, garrulous way...theatrically daring." *–The New Yorker.* [3W] ISBN: 0-8222-1843-7

★ **THE NINA VARIATIONS by Steven Dietz.** In this funny, fierce and heartbreaking homage to *The Seagull*, Dietz puts Chekhov's star-crossed lovers in a room and doesn't let them out. "A perfect little jewel of a play..." *–Shepherdstown Chronicle.* "...a delightful revelation of a writer at play; and also an odd, haunting, moving theater piece of lingering beauty." *–Eastside Journal (Seattle).* [1M, 1W (flexible casting)] ISBN: 0-8222-1891-7

DRAMATISTS PLAY SERVICE, INC.
440 Park Avenue South, New York, NY 10016 212-683-8960 Fax 212-213-1539
postmaster@dramatists.com www.dramatists.com